Dear Shirley

In anticipa

board appoin......

Laverne
3/6/2015

MW01485608

THE
BOARD OF DIRECTORS
AND
AUDIT COMMITTEE
GUIDE TO
FIDUCIARY
RESPONSIBILITIES

THE
BOARD OF DIRECTORS
AND
AUDIT COMMITTEE
GUIDE TO
FIDUCIARY RESPONSIBILITIES

Ten Critical Steps to Protecting Yourself and Your Organization

Sheila Moran, CPA, CFE, and Ronald Kral, CPA, CMA

AMACOM
American Management Association
New York • Atlanta • Brussels • Chicago • Mexico City • San Francisco
Shanghai • Tokyo • Toronto • Washington, D.C.

Bulk discounts available. For details visit:
www.amacombooks.org/go/specialsales
Or contact special sales:
Phone: 800-250-5308
Email: specialsls@amanet.org
View all the AMACOM titles at: www.amacombooks.org
American Management Association: www.amanet.org

This publication is designed to provide accurate and authoritative information in regard to the subject matter covered. It is sold with the understanding that the publisher is not engaged in rendering legal, accounting, or other professional service. If legal advice or other expert assistance is required, the services of a competent professional person should be sought.

Moran, Sheila.
  The board of directors and audit committee guide to fiduciary responsibilities : ten critical steps to protecting yourself and your organization / Sheila Moran, Ronald Kral.
    p.   cm.
  Includes index.
  ISBN 978-0-8144-3166-5 (hardcover) — ISBN 0-8144-3166-6 (hardcover)   1. Directors of corporations—Legal status, laws, etc.—United States.   2. Executives—Legal status, laws, etc.—United States.   3. Audit committees—Law and legislation—United States.   4. Corporate governance—Law and legislation—United States.   I. Kral, Ronald.   II. Title.

  KF1423.M67 2013
  657'.4580973—dc23
                                                        2013007791

© 2013 Sheila Moran
All rights reserved.
Printed in the United States of America.

This publication may not be reproduced, stored in a retrieval system, or transmitted in whole or in part, in any form or by any means, electronic, mechanical, photocopying, recording, or otherwise, without the prior written permission of AMACOM, a division of American Management Association, 1601 Broadway, New York, NY 10019.

  The scanning, uploading, or distribution of this book via the Internet or any other means without the express permission of the publisher is illegal and punishable by law. Please purchase only authorized electronic editions of this work and do not participate in or encourage piracy of copyrighted materials, electronically or otherwise. Your support of the author's rights is appreciated.

About AMA

American Management Association (www.amanet.org) is a world leader in talent development, advancing the skills of individuals to drive business success. Our mission is to support the goals of individuals and organizations through a complete range of products and services, including classroom and virtual seminars, webcasts, webinars, podcasts, conferences, corporate and government solutions, business books, and research. AMA's approach to improving performance combines experiential learning—learning through doing—with opportunities for ongoing professional growth at every step of one's career journey.

Printing number
10 9 8 7 6 5 4 3 2 1

CONTENTS

The
Board of
Directors
and
Audit Committee
Guide to
Fiduciary
Responsibilities

INTRODUCTION

IN THE WAKE of the 2001 collapses of Enron, WorldCom, and Arthur Andersen, professionals, lawmakers, and stakeholders alike turned their focus to issues such as corporate governance, accountability, and transparency, pushing C-suite executives, managers, and board members to more closely scrutinize the inner workings of businesses. In the decade since, however, corporate malfeasance has remained in the headlines, with attention-grabbing collapses of such corporate stalwarts as Lehman Brothers, which in 2008 accounted for the largest bankruptcy in U.S. history—and nearly brought down the entire U.S. economy.

According to the 2011 *Performance and Accountability Report* by the U.S. Securities and Exchange Commission (SEC), the SEC filed 735 enforcement actions covering a broad spectrum of financial wrongdoing during the fiscal year ended September 30, 2011.[1] This represented an 8.6 percent increase from 2010—more cases than ever previously filed by the SEC's Division of Enforcement in a single fiscal year. Those enforcement cases, and those from 2010, resulted in $3.6 billion in penalties and disgorgement (i.e., the repayment of illicit gains), with many of the financial wrongdoings falling under the general oversight of audit committee activities.

Despite some notable business failures and enormous fines, boards of directors have done much to improve the accountability and transparency of the companies they oversee. In fact, strong boards and audit committees can do—and have done—much to help build great companies. Because many organizations do not impanel a separate

1

audit committee, the entire board may be called upon to fulfill that function. Therefore, this book interchangeably uses the terms "board" and "audit committee."

In this era of closer scrutiny and larger fines, those who sit on boards and committees must do all they can to hold management accountable for its actions. In fact, regulators and disgruntled shareholders are accelerating their efforts to hold board directors personally accountable for their actions as well as for perceived inaction in their role in overseeing management, meaning that anyone who chooses to sit on a board or audit committee can be sued if the organization or directors break the law. Directors and committee members must be thorough, independent, and able to apply their expertise when overseeing organizations, whether public or private, for-profit or nonprofit.

No organization should harbor the false impression that the full board can carry on the duties of an audit committee without ample expertise at the board level. For example, Sonora Resources Corp. reported just such a material weakness to the SEC in an annual filing, stating, "We have a board which consists of the Chief Executive Officer and we do not have an audit committee. An audit committee would improve oversight in the establishment and monitoring of required internal controls and procedures."[2] Such material weakness points to both a lack of independence at the board level and a lack of expertise—something no organization should allow.

In another example, Buka Ventures Inc. reported a material weakness in an annual filing to the SEC, noting that "[c]ertain entity level controls establishing a 'tone at the top' were considered material weaknesses" and that the company "did not have a separate audit committee or a policy on fraud." The disclosure continues: "There is no system in place to review and monitor internal control over financial reporting. The Company maintains an insufficient complement of personnel to carry out ongoing monitoring responsibilities and ensure effective internal control over financial reporting."[3]

These examples point to a dangerous recipe for errors and fraud. Weak, ill-informed, and inexperienced boards and audit committees can contribute in many negative ways to the downfalls of organizations. On the other hand, strong boards and audit committees stand at the core of strong organizations.

The audit committee is responsible for overseeing internal and external audit functions, financial reporting, and disclosure. Any publicly traded company in the United States listed on a stock exchange must maintain a qualified audit committee whose members consist of independent outside directors, and disclose if they have at least one financial expert, or otherwise, to explain why they do not. The audit committee is the most commonly referred to standing committee of the board—and for good reason: This is the group of individuals that ensures primary oversight of an organization's financial reporting process and internal controls. As the board committee that is assigned primary responsibility to protect investor interests, the audit committee is a key component of the corporate governance structure. Yet failures and weaknesses in corporate governance arrangements are commonly cited as being behind business catastrophes, including the financial crisis of 2007–2008 that brought the world to the brink of economic chaos.

Boards of directors and audit committees must do all they can to ensure that proper corporate governance strategies are in place, that transparency is embedded in the organization's culture, and that financial reporting processes are followed to the letter. Successful board and audit committee members must:

> Understand and satisfy regulatory and legal expectations of board service.

> Equip themselves with tools to direct both internal and external auditors.

> Learn how to identify the leading financial reporting distortions.

> Find out how to build an effective team as a board and audit committee.

> Know what to ask when invited to join a board or committee.

> Protect stakeholder interests by reducing organizational exposure to adverse events through risk-management and fraud-deterrence activities.

> Prepare for bad news with a crisis media-action plan.

> Balance stakeholder interests concerning executive compensation and employee relations.

> Explore the effects of management influence over board oversight duties.

The Board of Directors and Audit Committee Guide to Fiduciary Responsibilities provides specific guidance that helps committee members satisfy the requirements of serving as board members while protecting themselves and their organizations. It offers practical advice to anyone who wants to fulfill his or her duties without adverse legal, reputational, or financial repercussions. Readers will find insight and actionable recommendations regarding the audit committee's role in management and audit oversight.

The book boils down the voluminous, highly technical guidance provided to board directors into ten easily understood and achieved action steps:

1. Nominate independent directors
2. Establish a culture of action
3. Evaluate the audit committee
4. Direct the external audit
5. Scrutinize the financial statements
6. Leverage internal audit and outside resources
7. Satisfy regulators and other stakeholders
8. Address risk proactively
9. Spearhead fraud-deterrence initiatives
10. Expect the unexpected

These ten actions should not be thought of as discrete, sequential steps. Rather, they cover essential topics that, when performed together, provide a composite set of governance strategies that give audit committee members and board directors the necessary peace of mind to know that they are fulfilling their at times daunting responsibilities. Each of these steps is equally important, with no consideration of value implied by the order in which they are presented.

Good governance by the audit committee is a game of endurance. It requires a systematic approach that must be continually updated and monitored to address emergent threats. As a director, you can be sure that scrutiny of the execution of director and audit committee duties will continue to increase in direct proportion to the level of the public's distrust of financial reporting.

This book presents an authoritative, reliable framework that audit committee and board members can follow to ensure that they are fulfilling their fiduciary responsibilities in a responsible yet efficient manner. By following the steps outlined, audit committee members can protect themselves and their fellow directors, as well as the company's reputation and stakeholder interests—most importantly those of shareholders.

CHAPTER ONE

Nominate Independent Directors

A WELL-RECRUITED AUDIT COMMITTEE provides a brain trust of backgrounds, experience, perceptions, intellect, and specific skills that facilitate cross-fertilization and exposure to new ideas. The audit committee is typically responsible for monitoring all internal and external audit functions of a company, overseeing the financial reporting process, and ensuring regulatory compliance. For publicly traded companies listed on a stock exchange, at least three independent directors are required to sit on the audit committee, with a requirement to disclose whether they have at least one financial expert.

Selecting members with an eye toward nurturing a culture that is collegial yet critical promotes the atmosphere of accountability necessary to ask hard questions of the chief financial officer, the external auditor, and even the chairman of the board and the organization's chief executive officer. This chapter presents considerations for the nominating committee and for audit committee candidates.

Nominating Committee Perspective

Audit committee success starts with the nomination process. Therefore, audit committee success ultimately rests on the shoulders of the full board of directors because the appointment of directors, including audit committee members, is a full board responsibility. The recruitment and selection of new directors and the evaluation of incumbent directors typically rests with the board's nominating committee, if one exists; otherwise the entire committee may take on the task of finding new members. The nominating committee is sometimes referred to as the corporate governance committee.

In considering candidates for open audit committee positions, nominating committees consider a candidate's independence, the need for a financial expert, diversity of skill sets, and demographic diversity.

Independence

The presence of independent oversight of management is directly linked to a lower perceived risk for the organization. An organization that lacks independent oversight is typically associated with a higher cost of capital because a potential shareholder or creditor demands a higher rate of return to compensate for the additional risk. So nominating committees strive to impanel an audit committee of which all members, or at least a majority, meet the organization's definition of independence. For public companies listed on stock exchanges, all members of the audit committee must be independent per the listing requirements of the exchanges in order to comply with Section 301 of the Sarbanes-Oxley Act of 2002 (SOX), which requires that all members of an audit committee be independent for public companies that are listed on a national securities exchange.

Director independence is a vastly deeper, wider, and more complex topic than can be described by strictly adhering to specific definitions, because of the informal nature of many social connections that could impair independence. Regulators have been challenged to articulate a definition of independence that goes beyond direct relationships to address the deep web of personal connections formed through neighborhoods, schools, fraternities, social clubs, gyms, industry associations, former board members, and the like.

Regulators and funding sources have provided a slew of definitions of independence in an attempt to promote an audit committee culture immune from conflict-of-interest risks. In the case of audit committees, it is especially important that directors are independent from those in management and from the external auditor over whom they watch. Let's take a look at the definition of related parties per U.S. generally accepted accounting principles (GAAP), legal definitions of independence, and practical definition considerations for nonpublic companies.

Related Parties per U.S. GAAP

Directors and audit committee members are forbidden from involving themselves in related-party transactions unless properly disclosed in the financial statements, as such events might give rise to conflicts of interest and inhibit the appearance of independence required for boards and committees.

U.S. GAAP, the collection of generally accepted accounting standards by the Financial Accounting Standards Board, offers a definition for related parties that includes *affiliates, control, immediate family, management, principal owners,* and other *related parties.* Although the technical definition for *related parties* is quite long, it boils down to a relationship that offers the potential for transactions that are conducted at less than arm's-length distance, that offer favorable treatment, or that provide an ability to influence the outcome of events differently from what might result in the absence of that relationship. U.S. GAAP goes on to stipulate that related-party transactions are not necessarily illegal, but material related-party transactions must be disclosed to the readers of the financial statements. Creditors of private companies and funding sources of nonprofit organizations require similar disclosures of related-party transactions, with the key objective of these disclosures being improved transparency of the relationships between the board, its audit committee, and management.[1]

Legal Definitions of Independence

As mentioned, Section 301 of SOX requires that for public companies listed on a national securities exchange, all members of an audit committee be independent. In order to be considered independent for purposes of SOX, audit committee members may not, other than in their capacity as directors, "(i) accept any consulting, advisory, or other compensatory fee from the issuer; or (ii) be an affiliated person of the issuer or any subsidiary thereof."

The SEC is tasked with crafting rules and regulations to effectively implement SOX. In doing so, the SEC directs companies to use the definition of independence from the national securities exchange or interdealer quotation system applicable to them.

All national securities exchanges and interdealer quotation systems in the United States have definitions of independence. For example, the New York Stock Exchange (NYSE) requires boards to affirmatively qualify directors as independent by determining that each director has no material relationship with the listed company. It further specifies that a director is not independent if the director:

> ➤ Is or has been within the past three years an employee of the listed company.

> ➤ Has an immediate family member who is or has been within the past three years an executive officer of the listed company.

> ➤ Accepts more than $120,000 in direct compensation (other than director fees) from the listed company.

> ➤ Is a current partner or employee of a firm that is the listed company's internal or external auditor.

> ➤ Has been within the past three years employed as an executive officer of another company where any of the listed company's present executive officers at the same time serves or served on that company's compensation committee.

> ➤ Is a current executive officer of a company that has sales or purchase transactions greater than $1 million or 2 percent to the other listed company's consolidated gross revenues.[2]

The NYSE definition also notes that "it is not possible to anticipate, or explicitly to provide for, all circumstances that might signal potential conflicts of interest, or that might bear on the materiality of a director's relationship to a listed company."[3] The NYSE definition makes it clear that it is in the best interest of boards to broadly make independence determinations to consider all relevant facts and circumstances. The board should consider independence not merely from the standpoint of the director, but also consider independence from the standpoint of persons or organizations with which the director has a relationship. These relationships can include commercial, industrial, banking, consulting, legal, accounting, charitable, and family ties.

The NASDAQ Stock Market (NASDAQ) has similar rules to the NYSE guidelines, but it allows for compensation up to only $60,000.

Those public companies not subject to listing requirements must adopt and disclose a definition of independence using one of the recognized definitions that listed companies use. The definition must be disclosed in annual filings to the SEC or posted on the company's website.

Practical Definition Considerations for Nonpublic Companies

The NYSE definition of independence can provide guidance to help any organization craft its own definition of independence for the purposes of recruiting strong audit committee members. No single definition is going to perfectly hit the mark for all types of organizations. Companies and nonprofit organizations operate in a diverse array of sizes and industries, each with its own risks.

A purist definition of an independent director or committee member is someone whose directorship constitutes his or her only connection to the organization. Boards are encouraged to use the definitions as a minimum because independence is in reality intangible and immeasurable, rather than something that can be captured by any rules-based definition, as attempted by the NYSE's definition. A good definition has elements of both a general guiding principle and certain well-defined parameters. Some organizations find it helpful to augment a general definition with specific examples of what does or does not constitute independence.

ACTION STEPS

▲ Avoid director candidates who have a direct financial connection to the organization.

▲ Be mindful of the impact of social relationships on independence.

▲ Craft an independence policy that provides a general definition of independence along with specific scenarios of independence and nonindependence.

Financial Expert

The term *financial expert* has entered into the vocabulary of mainstream corporate America in large part because of SOX.[4] Although it is not a requirement for nonpublic companies to have a financial expert on their audit committee, it is for publicly traded companies unless they disclose to the public why they do not. The criteria for what constitutes a financial expert should be strongly considered when recruiting audit committee members.

The SEC and SOX define an audit committee financial expert to be a person who has the following attributes:

> An understanding of generally accepted accounting principles and financial statements

> The ability to assess the general application of such principles in connection with the accounting for estimates, accruals, and reserves

> Experience preparing, auditing, analyzing, or evaluating financial statements that present a breadth and level of complexity of accounting issues that are generally comparable to the breadth and complexity of issues that can reasonably be expected to be raised by the company they serve

> An understanding of internal controls over financial reporting (ICFR), that is, those controls that are designed

and that function to provide assurance that the output of the financial reporting system is accurate and complete

➤ An understanding of audit committee functions[5]

The SEC's Final Disclosure Rules Regarding Audit Committee Financial Experts requires that the financial expert, if one or more exists, be identified in a filing. While the SEC does not require publicly traded companies to have a financial expert on the audit committee, the failure to have at least one requires disclosure, including an explanation why no such expert is included in the audit committee. This disclosure requirement operates in practice as a de facto requirement to have at least one financial expert on the audit committee because companies do not wish to been seen as not having financial expertise on the committee. Some organizations have multiple financial experts on their audit committee.

National securities exchanges have audit committee requirements that go beyond that of SOX or the SEC. For example, the NYSE requires that all members of the audit committee for public companies listed on the NYSE be financially literate.[6] While what is required to be classified as "financially literate" is left to the interpretation of the listed company, it is widely viewed as being comfortable with the basics of GAAP and proficient in reading financial statements prepared in accordance with GAAP.

An ongoing convergence of accounting standards between GAAP and International Financial Reporting Standards has been widely hailed as a principle-based GAAP. Wise discernment by audit committee members regarding an appropriate interpretation of the international standards only increases the need for financially astute members of the audit committee.

Diversity of Skill Sets

Organizations benefit from having directors who bring a diverse set of skills, expertise, and backgrounds that yield a varied approach to decision making. That said, because organizations can hire specialized expertise as needs warrant, it is not necessary to fulfill the complete wish list of skill sets in the audit committee recruitment process. Some common areas in which audit committee members may be asked to roll up their sleeves and contribute their expertise include:

> Regulatory: Organizations of all industries and sizes need to keep abreast of constant changes to the regulatory landscape. Audit committee members with regulatory experience can help guide the necessary updates to the organization's policies and procedures.

> Supply chain: An understanding of the company's suppliers and what options exist for the industry is essential not just for board members at large but also for audit committees, which must assess the reasonableness of variations in organizational performance related to vendor pricing.

> Marketing and branding: Because marketing and branding can have an impact on revenues and profitability, it can be helpful to have an audit committee member who can step in and help the chief executive officer (CEO) or the chief operating officer (COO) evaluate the impact of marketing and branding strategies on the statement of operations.

> Information security: The growing risks associated with the proliferation of information and the associated potential for insider trading makes information security an increasingly sensitive area for most organizations. Because the chief information officer usually reports to the chief financial officer (CFO), and because what the CFO does is under the watchful eye of the audit committee, it can be a natural fit for audit committee members to weigh in on technology matters.

> Risk management: Strategic, operational, financial reporting, and compliance risks, while often owned by management, need to be overseen at the board level. The audit committee should have the topic of risk on every meeting agenda, and members should challenge management as to proper identification, assessment, and management of the risks (see Chapter 8).

> ➤ International business experience: The world is getting smaller from a business standpoint as more industries consolidate through mergers and acquisitions. If a company's current operations are international, or if there are plans to grow internationally, this can be an area of great advisory need where the insights of an audit committee member can be quite valuable.

Demographic Diversity

In addition to diversity of skill sets, it is also helpful to consider diversity in demographics. Renee Adams and Daniel Ferreira report in their article "Women in the Boardroom and Their Impact on Governance and Performance," published in the *Journal of Financial Economics*, that there was "direct evidence that more diverse boards are more likely to hold CEOs accountable for poor stock price performance."[7]

Despite the benefits of demographic diversity, it remains a challenge for boards and audit committees. The *2011 Spencer Stuart Board Index* reported that while women and minorities are still underrepresented, their representation on boards is improving, with women "accounting for just over 16% of all independent directors, up from 12% in 2001."[8] The index did show a "small decline in the share of African-American directors" but an increase in Hispanic/Latino and Asian directors.

Improving demographic diversity could be one way to help promote effective audit committee operations. Management oversight is a key role of audit committee and board members, and different people with different backgrounds bring different perspectives to boards and committees, which may lead to improved oversight and accountability.

ACTION STEPS

▲ Recruit audit committee members who are financially literate, with at least one financial expert on the audit committee.

▲ Look to expand the organization's wealth of knowledge by recruiting audit committee members with diverse skill sets.

▲ Consider demographic diversity as a way to enhance management oversight.

Candidate Perspective

Now let's shift from the discussion of selecting audit committee members to the matter of becoming an audit committee member.

Landing one's first board directorship is a career milestone. Qualified candidates can expect a board placement at an S&P 500 company to yield on average $232,000 in director compensation, according to the *2011 Spencer Stuart Board Index*.[9] Serving as audit committee chairman pays a premium, with retainers in the range of $5,000 to $100,000.[10]

Once a director demonstrates proven skills, more offers to serve on boards typically follow. However, while many directors serve on more than one board, the Spencer Stuart index reports that there are increasing restrictions on serving on multiple boards, with "74% of S&P 500 companies now limiting other corporate directorships for their board members." Furthermore, the Spencer Stuart index reports that "40% of boards limit other audit committee memberships for their own audit committee members," with most organizations that place limits on directors serving on multiple audit committees restricting the maximum number of audit committee appointments to two.[11] Given that situation, candidates should be selective in the board directorships and audit committee assignments they accept.

In evaluating an appointment as an audit committee or board member, candidates should start by requesting:

> ➤ A copy of the board policy manual with a list of responsibilities of the board members, description of committees, and their charter statements.

> ➤ Audit committee meeting minutes for the previous eighteen months (or whatever period of time seems appropriate given the circumstances of the organization).

Questions Candidates Can Ask

In addition to making document requests, candidates can talk to the CFO, external auditor, other directors, and former directors. When speaking to former directors, be aware of biases. Vicki Medvec of the Center for Executive Women at Northwestern University finds that candidates, especially first-time board members, often don't ask enough questions. Here are some suggestions from Medvec and Georgia Nelson of the Center for Executive Women for talking with current and former directors:

> ➤ Ask for an example of a time when the board did not agree and how that was resolved. Be wary if members say there have been no disagreements.

> ➤ Ask about past regulatory issues and/or sanctions.

> ➤ Ask what they perceive to be the risks in the industry.

> ➤ Ask what they consider to be robust debate, and ask for an example. Investigate whether discussions include active debate.

> ➤ Ask to see safety records, which is of particular importance for audit committee members who have regulatory oversight and need to be aware of Occupational Safety and Health Administration–type regulations.

> ➤ Ask to see the values statement for the workforce.

> ➤ Ask about turnover and employee-based class action suits.

Medvec and Nelson also suggest reading the company's blog. The ultimate goal is to get information from multiple sources.

Prospective board and committee members may find that the organization has outdated corporate governance practices. For example, the board policy manual may have last been updated fifteen years ago. While unfortunate, such circumstances do occur. The key to deciding if the organization is a worthy investment of time, effort, and reputation is in understanding the organization's desire to change. A conversation with the chairman of the board and the CEO about the organization's ability to update the board policy manual and committee charters to reflect the current structure and operation of the board and its committees may be in order. Good questions to ask the CEO include "What do you see as the role of the board?" and "What is your relationship to the board?" If it is clear that the board and the CEO have an effective and ethical culture, or at least the willingness to build such a culture, an organization with outdated corporate governance practices may still be worth consideration.

ACTION STEPS

▲ Be selective when accepting board and committee appointments.

▲ Ask probing questions of current and former directors, as well as the external auditor.

▲ Don't be alarmed if the organization has outdated corporate governance procedures.

▲ Follow up with the CEO and board chairman to assess the organization's readiness to evolve.

Chapter Two

Establish a Culture of Action

An effective audit committee serves as a gatekeeper, protecting the long-term interests of shareholders and its other important constituencies, such as creditors, regulators, employees, customers, suppliers, and the public, as may be applicable. Succeeding as a committee depends on understanding the expectations as well as the essential competencies required of audit committees and their members.

Expectations of Audit Committees

The precise steps audit committees take to fulfill their duties is dictated by the expectations of audit committee members and all board directors, so clarifying the goals and outcomes of committee action is crucial. Those expectations are shaped, at a minimum, by four basic fiduciary duties: care, loyalty, obedience, and oversight.

Duty of Care

Audit committee members must act with the care that a "reasonably prudent person" in a similar position would use under similar circumstances. The reasonably prudent person doctrine, also known as the reasonable man test, has emerged as a way of determining legal negligence and asks juries to evaluate the actions of a defendant based on the expected response and actions of a person by the standards that develop within a community of peers.

In short, duties must be performed in good faith and in the best interest of the company. The duty of care rests upon the principle of stewardship in that directors must make decisions such that organizational resources are preserved and, if possible, enhanced.

The business judgment rule that demands that directors make decisions in good faith and for the benefit of the organization can aid directors who must defend their decision making under attacks that they did not fulfill the duty of care. Because directors are not expected to possess complete financial acumen to adequately serve, audit committee members and board directors can hire outside resources to ensure that decisions are well informed.

Duty of Loyalty

Duty of loyalty addresses the need of audit committee members and board directors to make decisions free of conflicts of interests. The duty of loyalty gives rise to the sole purpose doctrine, which requires audit committee members to put the best interest of the company and its shareholders ahead of any interest possessed by any individual director.

Under the principle of duty of loyalty, directors cannot make use of corporate assets, opportunities, or information for personal gain. Insider trading and certain related-party transactions that unduly enrich directors are prohibited by the duty of loyalty.

Insider trading has brought down the illustrious careers of many professionals, including that of Goldman Sachs director Rajat Gupta. Gupta ran McKinsey & Co. from 1994 to 2003 and was a director at both Goldman Sachs and Procter & Gamble. Gupta was convicted in 2012 of leaking tips regarding Goldman Sachs and Procter & Gamble to Raj Rajaratnam, a hedge fund manager. Among the alleged secrets revealed was information Gupta shared with Rajaratnam that Procter & Gamble intended to sell a subsidiary, Folgers Coffee, to Smucker. In this case, the duty of loyalty placed on directors was breached because Gupta violated an implied loyalty of confidentiality that allowed an individual, Rajaratnam, rather than shareholders at large, to benefit from private information that if openly known could have led to wider gains in the market.

Duty of Obedience

Duty of obedience requires audit committee members to perform their duties in accordance with applicable laws and the terms of their board's charter. With the duty of obedience, boards and their committees are restrained from capricious application of board and committee charters.

Duty of Oversight

The duty of oversight requires audit committee members to be proactive in ensuring that they have full and necessary information for performing their duties. This duty includes the responsibility to ensure that the company has adequate ICFR in place resulting in the preparation and publication of timely, accurate, and comprehensive financial statements.

Directors who ignore situations or transactions that put the organization at risk, or do not research them with care, could be personally liable. To successfully attack directors for lack of oversight, the plaintiff must show three things:

1. The director knew, or should have known, of the violation.
2. The director did nothing to remedy the problem.
3. The lack of oversight caused damages.

The business judgment rule under the duty of care can stave off charges of inaction under the duty of oversight as long as directors discuss emergent problems, even if the problem is later deemed trivial, with such discussions documented in the board and/or committee minutes.

These duties apply to all organizations, for-profit and nonprofit, public and private. Although nonprofits do not have shareholders as part of the stakeholder group, directors of nonprofits have funding sources, which can include government agencies, foundations, and individuals. These stakeholders expect directors to execute their role with the duties of care, loyalty, obedience, and oversight.

Privately held businesses have shareholders, as do publicly traded businesses, but because most stock is closely held (i.e., have a limited number of shareholders), a misconception can exist that fiduciary expectations are lower. However, courts have found that other stakeholders, such as creditors, have the rightful expectation that the directors fulfill the duties of loyalty, care, obedience, and oversight.

This point is highlighted in the case of *Pereira v. Cogan*,[1] which involved a privately held corporation called Trace International Holdings Inc. Marshall Cogan controlled Trace as its majority shareholder, CEO, and chairman of the board. Cogan had installed his friends as officers and directors and proceeded to pillage the company by paying himself excessively through illegal dividends, inappropriate loans, and an illegal share buy-back transaction. The suit, brought by John Pereira as trustee of Trace International Holdings Inc., charged the company's officers and directors along with Cogan because they did not prevent Cogan's looting of the company assets. The court found that the directors' lack of due diligence, which demands that directors act with certain standards of care, constituted a breach of the fiduciary duties of loyalty and care owed to Trace's creditors. The court held the directors personally liable for more than $40 million in improper transactions.[2]

ACTION STEPS

- ▲ Use outside resources when necessary to ensure decisions are well informed.

- ▲ Consider all stakeholders, not just shareholders, when making decisions in the best interest of the organization.

- ▲ Document discussions to ensure the business judgment rule can be asserted against claims over lack of oversight.

Essential Audit Committee Proficiencies

To effectively execute the duties of the board and its committees, audit committee members should strive to promote proficiency in the following areas:

- Governance structure
- Culture
- Independence
- Access to information and dissemination
- Management oversight
- Orientation and training
- Shareholder and other stakeholder relations

Governance Structure

Governance relates to the set of processes, policies, and institutions that affect how an organization is controlled and directed. Board bylaws, committee charters, and corporate governance documents, collectively known as policies and procedures at the board level, work together to outline the board's plan to fulfill its commitment to proper oversight of the financial reporting process, including those responsibilities specifically designed to address the expectations of the external auditor. These policies and procedures tend to evolve over time in response to changes in the organization's environment. Because of this, organizations should periodically review their charter and other governance documents. Audit committee charters and other governance documents should include language that:

- Empowers the audit committee to approve financial statements and to hire or fire the external auditor.
- Specifies the reporting chain between the audit committee and the chairman of the board, and/or lead director if one has been appointed, as well as with the CFO, external auditor, and internal auditor.

> ➤ Gives the audit committee authority, without having to seek board approval, to obtain advice from outside advisers. The audit committee needs to be in control of its own funding, with complete autonomy over its budget.

> ➤ Sets meeting protocols, in terms of frequency, quorum, and forum. Although most jurisdictions allow directors to take action by unanimous written consent, this procedure should not replace face-to-face meetings. Meeting protocols should include provisions for meeting by telephone or videoconference.

ACTION STEPS

▲ As a matter of good governance, be sure that the audit committee has the ability to hire its own advisers, including the external auditor.

▲ Be sure the audit committee has a direct reporting line to the chairman of the board and/or the lead director if one is appointed.

▲ Ensure that audit committee charters and related governance documents establish proper meeting protocols.

Culture

Audit committee cultures are as divergent as human nature. Even so, audit committees universally benefit from operating with the confidence, trust, and respect among committee members that typically develop from certain traits, including a collegial yet critical spirit. Such an approach requires a willingness to challenge each other and management. Special attention may be needed to avoid groupthink, which is the natural tendency of groups to minimize conflict for the sake of harmony. Groupthink can result in decisions being made without critical discussion of alternative viewpoints.

Open access to agendas and discussions are crucial to the success of audit committees and boards of directors. Vicki Medvec of the Center for Executive Women at Northwestern University instructs board members to ask key questions such as, "Who controls discussions?"

and "Is there a favored director?" when assessing the culture of the board and its committees.

Sensitivity to understanding the culture of the organization at large also is crucial. Although the board is responsible for setting the tone at the top (i.e., the organization's ethical culture as defined by the board of directors and senior management), the tone at the middle is an important gauge in evaluating the effectiveness of the culture of the board and its committees. Medvec and Georgia Nelson of the Center for Executive Women suggest evaluating the ethical culture by, among other things, looking at rewards and organizational responses to whistle-blower hotlines (see Chapter 9 for appropriate responses to such hotlines) to evaluate the effectiveness of board-initiated efforts to promote an ethical culture throughout an organization. In considering the influence of rewards, board and audit committee members can ask who gets the rewards. As for responses to hotlines and other venues by which complaints are voiced, audit committee members should ensure that reports of fraud and, for example, toxic managers, be addressed swiftly and appropriately. Such actions exemplify accountability.

ACTION STEPS

▲ Be on the lookout for groupthink in an effort to promote the consideration of opposing viewpoints in decision making.

▲ Strive to provide members equal time during discussions.

▲ Be sensitive to how culture lives throughout the organization, beyond the dictates and practices of the board.

▲ Engage management by providing insights in the process of executing the board's duty of management oversight.

▲ Offer routine training to new and continuing audit committee members.

▲ Promote open communications with stakeholders, complying with required reporting and disclosure standards.

Independence

Independence is a desirable trait in audit committees and board directors because it implies that decisions can be made regardless of self-serving interests. Effective director recruitment sets the stage for independent decision making (see Chapter 1). Even so, independence in board and committee operations should continue to be evaluated. As mentioned, many boards require that audit committee members be independent of all related-party transactions, while other boards set the standard that audit committee members must abstain from any discussions and votes when they are conflicted from acting in an unbiased and objective manner.

Access to Information and Dissemination

Decisions made by audit committee members are only as good as the information they are provided. Optimal information flow involves information exchanges in all directions. In addition, healthy and productive information flow requires deep scrutiny of the level of detail of the information reported. Too much information can be crippling.

To improve the digestibility of data presented, special attention must be made in designing board packets so that reports provide actionable data that is highlighted and brought to the forefront. A dashboard reporting tool, which summarizes key information across commonly defined and understood terms, is a popular reporting format. Those directors who prefer copious data can be assured that more detailed information can be available upon request.

ACTION STEPS

▲ Be conscious of independence concerns, having conflicted directors abstain from votes that appear to lack objectivity.

▲ Pay attention to information flow, removing blockages and improving board reporting for improved absorption and response.

▲ Ask for additional information as necessary when situations warrant.

Management Oversight

A key duty of the audit committee is oversight of the CEO and CFO in order to verify that management is adequately performing its duties. In addition to providing an oversight function for external stakeholders, audit committees can add value to the organization by providing the CFO with advice on a range of topics, including financial reporting, ICFR, risks, compliance, and regulatory disclosures.

A lack of healthy skepticism by the audit committee can deprive organizations and shareholders of the necessary oversight of management. Take, for example, the case of Corus Bankshares Inc. In 2012, Corus settled for $10 million a complaint alleging that the company issued materially false and misleading statements, failed to recognize losses on its condominium loans in accordance with U.S. GAAP, and purchased condominiums in developments it had financed in an attempt to inflate prices and sales.[3] When the company released financial results that brought to light its sales troubles, its stock value dropped sharply, and it declared bankruptcy. A deficiency in audit committee oversight of management made the misstatement of financial statements by Corus possible.

Orientation and Training

Training for new and existing audit committee members should never be taken for granted. Directors need training just like any other professionals. This is especially critical for new independent audit committee members who need to be oriented to the company culture, stakeholders, governance guidelines, competition, and in some cases industry. Continuing audit committee members also benefit from routine training to keep abreast of changing laws and regulations, new accounting standards, stakeholder initiatives, new auditing standards, and industry developments. A good practice for new and continuing board members is to periodically visit operational divisions and undergo facility tours to get a firsthand look at operations.

Shareholder and Other Stakeholder Relations

Audit committees serve many masters, including shareholders, regulators, creditors, and vendors. Audit committee members must ensure that all disclosures to outside parties are properly supported, factual, timely, and verified for legal compliance. Transparency can be tricky because audit committee members must keep a great deal of information private, concealing information that may be proprietary. Yet there is a competing need to be open with financial information in order to be helpful to stakeholders. There is a tradeoff between candor and required confidentiality: Sharing too much information can impair the company's competitive position. As a result, for many boards, disclosure is limited to those communications specified by laws and regulations.

ACTION STEPS

▲ Engage management by providing insights into the process of executing the board's duty of management oversight.

▲ Offer routine training to new and continuing audit committee members.

▲ Promote open communications with stakeholders, complying with required reporting and disclosure standards.

CHAPTER THREE

Evaluate the Audit Committee

AUDIT COMMITTEES are facing increased scrutiny from share-holders and regulators for the manner in which they fulfill their duties, which stems from the public perception that they were somehow misled by the financial information presented prior to the deep economic recession that started in 2008. A well-designed audit committee evaluation can stave off critics and serve as a valuable tool for the full board of directors to help assess the success of one of their key standing committees. This chapter addresses the why, who, when, what, and how of conducting sound audit committee evaluations.

Why Should Evaluations Be Considered?

Regulatory requirements do not mandate that organizations undertake performance evaluations of their boards and board committees. Even so, nearly all boards annually evaluate the performance of the full board, with only 2 percent of S&P 500 boards choosing not to conduct some kind of annual performance evaluation, according to the *2011 Spencer Stuart Board Index*.[1] In addition, more than half examine the full board as well as individual committees.[2]

The NYSE is one of the few organizations to require evaluations of audit committees. The NYSE requires "an annual performance evaluation of the audit committee" for all public companies listed on its exchange.[3] This requirement must be written into the company's audit committee charter. However, the NYSE does not define the annual performance evaluation process. As a result, some listed NYSE companies have interpreted it as simply conducting annual internal discussions about their performance during an audit committee meeting and then documenting such discussions in the committee minutes. Other companies have defined the requirement as a much more rigorous evaluation process led by attorneys or independent third-party experts.

Whether performance evaluation routines are mandated or not, organizations of all types and from all industries should consider incorporating them into their process. While many tools exist for evaluating audit committees (many of which can be sourced from third-party service providers), some evaluation tools limit evaluations to the consideration of just the most basic fiduciary or regulatory requirements. Boards that go deeper in their evaluations enjoy many benefits, including:

> Accountability to each other and to stakeholders.

> Affirmation that duties are understood and accepted.

> Thorough consideration of independence among the audit committee, management, and external auditor.

> Confirmation that priorities align with organizational goals.

> Built-in process improvement through systematic reflection of what is working and what is not.

> Enhanced ability to attract and retain qualified audit committee members.

> Reduced cost of capital by improving stakeholder confidence.

ACTION STEPS

▲ Ensure that an annual review requirement is written into the audit committee's charter.

▲ View the evaluation as an opportunity to help mitigate regulatory and fiduciary risk.

▲ Articulate compelling reasons for the evaluation beyond compliance.

Who Is Best Positioned to Conduct the Evaluation?

Boards and audit committees have a choice when deciding who conducts the evaluations, whether it be internal resources such as C-suite executives, internal auditors, legal counsel, or even members of the board, or third parties such as outside counsel, individual consultants, specialty board consulting firms, or executive search firms. The party assigned the responsibility for performing the evaluation assists the board in processing surveys, questionnaires, and other documentation used for the evaluation. While most boards perform evaluations, the majority do them internally. The *2011 Spencer Stuart Board Index* reports that "only 14% [of boards] engage a third party to conduct board and/or director evaluations."[4]

Because the responsibility to conduct the evaluation requires access to confidential information, those assigned to perform evaluations should be mindful of the highly sensitive nature of the project. If an outside vendor is utilized, tight nondisclosure agreements need to be put in place, either by general counsel or outside legal representation.

Another important consideration is discoverability (i.e., the ability of documents to be subpoenaed) under laws and regulations of sensitive information collected during the evaluations. Organizations do not want to leave a long audit trail of the strengths and weaknesses of the audit committee, the board, or any board committee, because of potential legal exposure. To mitigate this risk, attorney–client privilege can be invoked by having either general counsel or outside counsel direct the evaluation. One established legal alternative when utilizing a nonattorney resource is to promptly destroy all records associated with the evaluation, consistent with a company-adopted records retention policy, other than noting in meeting minutes that it occurred. This can be a safe avenue to take once detailed results have been verbally delivered to the board and audit committee.

When Should Evaluations Be Performed?

For public companies listed on its exchange, the NYSE requires annual evaluations. At this time, NASDAQ does not require board evaluations. However, for smaller, less complex organizations, performing evaluations every other year is likely sufficient. The precise time frame should be dictated by the size and needs of the organization. Companies are well advised to adopt and stick to a periodic time frame. Failure to schedule evaluations can lead to continual postponement of the evaluation in lieu of other priorities.

More frequent evaluations may be dictated by special situations, such as a merger or acquisition, divestiture, or aggressive expansion into new markets. Under these scenarios, it often makes sense to undertake a special evaluation of the full board and its committees, including the audit committee, to assess its readiness for the new activity. These evaluations can be tailored and streamlined to meet specific needs of what lies ahead. A successful evaluation can help the organization identify needs and resources that the audit committee may not otherwise have considered under normal operations.

ACTION STEPS

▲ Consult an attorney to confirm that evaluations are performed and documented in such a way that sensitive data are not discoverable under law.

▲ Decide on a periodic time frame for the evaluation, and comply.

▲ Consider additional evaluations if circumstances, such as a merger or acquisition, warrant.

What Should Be Evaluated?

Companies have a lot of latitude on which areas they evaluate. Audit committees should strive to evaluate the more substantive aspects of performance, such as culture, independence, and relationships, which go beyond mere compliance items. The following provide a good basis for questions that can be asked during the evaluation process:

> ➤ Does the audit committee discharge the duties prescribed in the audit committee charter, such as compliance with legal requirements that arise out of credit agreements, stock exchange listing requirements, regulatory approvals, strategic initiatives such as merger and acquisition activities, and governmental filings?

> ➤ Does the audit committee exemplify the essential audit committee proficiencies outlined in Chapter 2, specifically, governance structure, culture, independence, access to information and dissemination, management oversight, orientation and training, and shareholder and other stakeholder relations?

> ➤ Are discussions well facilitated, with all members participating in discussions? Is there a good balance between presentation and discussion during meetings?

> ➤ Do all members have the ability to help craft the agenda?

> ➤ Are committee members satisfied with how conflict is resolved? Are dissent and disagreement with other directors, the CEO, and the CFO discouraged?

> ➤ Is the audit committee comfortable with the timeliness, accuracy, and comprehensiveness of information used to support key decisions?

> ➤ How early does management include the board and audit committee in the strategy-development process? Does management make a habit of bringing fully formed strate-

gies to the board for approval rather than engaging the
board for input earlier in the strategy-development
process?[5]

> Does risk receive sufficient attention in audit committee
discussions? Is risk a separate topic of discussion during
regular audit committee meetings? Is the audit committee
involved in developing the organization's risk appetite, and
is it invited to challenge management's risk-assessment
assumptions?

> Does the audit committee feel comfortable utilizing exter-
nal resources in carrying out its duties?

In addition to evaluating the audit committee as a whole, boards
can evaluate the performance of individual committee members, with
34 percent of boards doing so, according to the *2011 Spencer Stuart
Board Index*.[6] Evaluations of the audit committee can be conducted in
a similar fashion as evaluations of the board as a whole.

Negative responses to the questions above may indicate areas
of misunderstanding, areas of disagreement, or areas in need of
improvement. If misunderstanding or disagreement is uncovered,
members should discuss the issues in light of the committee's charter and duties. If any deficiencies are discovered among the committee as a whole or among individual committee members, the
audit committee and the board should discuss options for improving
on weaknesses.

ACTION STEPS

▲ Use the evaluation process to systemize the periodic consideration
of the audit committee's success in executing its fundamental duties.

▲ Address topics in the evaluation that relate to how the group makes
decisions.

▲ Consider evaluating individual directors as well as the committee as
a whole.

How Should the Evaluation Be Performed?

There is a great deal of scalability and flexibility in the precise design and implementation of evaluations, allowing an organization to design an evaluation process that suits its own complexity and budget. In addition, there are numerous evaluation methods from which to choose, such as checklists, surveys, one-on-one interviews, group discussions, or a blend of these tools.

Each method provides its own benefits. For example, the anonymous component of checklists and surveys can help protect the identities of respondents, which may foster more candid responses. Checklists with open-ended questions designed to bring to the surface issues that can spark group discussions about recurrent weaknesses can be particularly effective.

In addition to or as part of the formal evaluation process, Vicki Medvec and Georgia Nelson of the Center for Executive Women at Northwestern University suggest annual one-on-one conversations between the chairman and each member to solicit individual feedback. They also advise audit committees to conclude the evaluation process with an internal discussion lasting no more than an hour, if expediency is desired, and to consider the effectiveness of the evaluation process. Nelson and Medvec also recommend that audit committees ask key questions, such as, "What did we learn from the evaluation process?" and "What can we do to improve the evaluation process?" during the assessment of the evaluation process.

The board should consider what corrective action should be taken in response to any deficiencies identified by the evaluations.

ACTION STEPS

▲ Take advantage of the full variety of evaluation tools available to provide a full-bodied analysis of the health of the audit committee operations.

▲ Craft questionnaires thoughtfully to promote engaging discussions among committee members.

▲ Allow for time at the end of the evaluation process to consider improvements to the evaluation tools selected.

CHAPTER FOUR

Direct the External Audit

OVERSEEING THE EXTERNAL audit relationship, from hiring to firing, is one of the fundamental responsibilities of audit committees. The effort expended by audit committee members in this matter can play a crucial role in reducing the possibility of material misstatements. Material misstatements lead to restatements of financial statements, which often trigger class action lawsuits. For example, New Century Financial Corp. allegedly made false and misleading statements and omissions concerning its operations and financial results. Upon the company's disclosure in 2007 that the U.S. attorney's office was conducting a criminal inquiry and investigating accounting issues, New Century's stock price collapsed. Company executives, directors, and their external auditors subsequently became defendants in a class-action lawsuit, which resulted in a settlement of $124,827,088, of which external auditor KPMG LLP contributed $44,750,000.[1]

Many companies continue to struggle with this responsibility, not fully understanding how to direct the external audit to maximize value from it, the benefits of which can extend beyond meeting minimum regulatory compliance goals. This results in a lost opportunity to leverage the external auditor in helping to fulfill directors' duties. To maximize benefits of the external audit, audit committee members should be familiar with:

> ➤ The external audit process.

> ➤ Potential roles of the auditor.

> ➤ Hiring, evaluating, and replacing the external auditor.

The External Audit Process

The audit process can be viewed as three separate stages: preparation, fieldwork, and report writing. Preparation can begin several months before the fiscal year-end, with the external auditor setting up testing of ICFR and significant accounts, such as receivables and inventory. Internal control testing includes a review of the internal control processes and testing of certain controls to ensure that controls are operating as designed. Verifying receivables may require confirmations with customers that typically require a long lead time to ensure ample time for responses. As part of audit preparation, the auditor may also coordinate the timing of the physical inventory count.

The second stage, fieldwork, can take as little as one to two weeks and requires on-site testing that allows for interaction with staff and access to records. Fieldwork is generally scheduled four to eight weeks after year-end. The final stage, report writing, involves resolution of any matters not completed during fieldwork. At many organizations, the audit report is issued no later than 120 days after the fiscal year-end.

Leveraging the external audit process, including the resulting auditor's report, plays a central role in helping the audit committee fulfill its duties. It begins with education. Every director should be well versed on the value the external auditor can bring to the directors' table, as well as the risks. Specifically, audit committee members should be conversant with:

> ➤ The financial statement opinion.

> ➤ External audit standards.

> ➤ Auditor risk standards.

The Financial Statement Opinion

Audited financial statements contain management's financial statements and the external auditor's opinion on those statements to provide a high level of assurance that they are presented fairly, in all material respects, within generally accepted accounting principles.

The goal for all organizations is to receive an unqualified, or clean, opinion. A clean audit opinion indicates that the auditor believes there were no material errors in the financial statements. If an unqualified opinion cannot be issued, the auditor may qualify its opinion, issue an adverse opinion, or render a disclaimer of opinion, which occurs when the auditor cannot form any opinion at all. An auditor would use a qualified opinion to express concern about a significant limitation on the scope of the external auditor's work or a material departure in the financial statements from GAAP. Use of an adverse opinion is reserved for material GAAP departures or when there are multiple GAAP departures. An adverse opinion implies that the auditor considers the financial statements to be unreliable.

Although the auditor clearly plays an important function, over-reliance on external audit activities to detect errors and irregularities has come to haunt many audit committees. It should be noted that more fraud is detected through tips, management reviews, internal auditors, and even by accident than by external auditors, according to survey results from the 2012 *Report to the Nations on Occupational Fraud and Abuse* as published by the Association of Certified Fraud Examiners, a trade organization for antifraud professionals with more than 55,000 members in 125 countries. (See Chapter 5 for more details about how audit committees can scrutinize the financial statements.)

External Audit Standards

Only external auditors of publicly traded companies must adhere to audit committee requirements of the Public Company Accounting Oversight Board (PCAOB), created in 2002 with the passage of SOX. But all organizations subject to an external audit have the performance of their audit committee judged to some extent. External auditors of nonpublic companies are required to assess how the audit committee contributes to the organization's overall ICFR under standards established by the Auditing Standards Board of the American Institute of Certified Public Accountants (AICPA).

These external audit standards effectively require the auditor to evaluate the adequacy of communications with the audit committee. The auditor needs to conclude if the audit committee and its related communications were adequate to support the objective of the audit. If the auditor concludes that the oversight of the company's external financial reporting and ICFR by the company's audit committee is ineffective, the auditor must communicate that information in writing to the board of directors.[2]

Audit committee members must not take formal communications with the auditor lightly, as though it were just a simple formality. Too many audit committees let this annual ritual pass without taking advantage of its spirit. All sets of external audit standards have some degree of required communications. For example, consider the Auditing Standards Board's Statement on Auditing Standards No. 114, "The Auditor's Communication with Those Charged with Governance." This standard defines those charged with governance as "the person(s) with responsibility for overseeing the strategic direction of the entity and obligations related to the accountability of the entity."[3] For organizations with a board of directors, this term refers to them or to the audit committee. Required communications are:

1. The auditor's responsibilities under generally accepted auditing standards.
2. An overview of the planned scope and timing of the audit.
3. Significant findings from the audit.[4]

These required communications between the auditor and the audit committee provide a great opportunity for audit committee members to tune in and probe beyond what the auditor may initially communicate. While each of these three required communications is important, the third carries important considerations the auditor should communicate in the following matters:

> Views about qualitative aspects of the entity's significant accounting practices, including accounting policies, accounting estimates, and financial statement disclosures

> Significant difficulties encountered during the audit, including significant delays in management providing required information, unexpected effort required to obtain sufficient appropriate audit evidence, the unavailability of expected information, and any restrictions imposed on the auditors by management

> Uncorrected misstatements, other than those the auditor believes are trivial

> Disagreements with management

Robust communication on these matters can be enlightening for the auditor and the audit committee.

The auditor must base the evaluation on observations resulting from audit committee interactions throughout the audit process. This sounds reasonable, but remember that it is the audit committee that hires the auditor. Therefore, the requirement to have the auditor evaluate the group that hires it creates a similar concern about conflict of interest that existed between management and the auditor prior to SOX, when management had a more dominant role in the hiring of the auditor.

The auditor's assessment of the audit committee's effectiveness includes the auditor's consideration of the:

> Appropriateness and timeliness of actions taken by the audit committee in response to matters raised by the auditor.

> Openness of the audit committee in its communications with the auditor.

> Willingness and capacity of the audit committee to meet with the auditor without management present.

> Extent to which the audit committee probes issues raised by the auditor.

While most financial statements are audited for conformance to some form of GAAP, the specific external audit standards can vary based on industry and type of organization, such as nonprofits, publicly traded companies, governments, or private companies. These standards include:

> AICPA Auditing Standards
> Public Company Accounting Oversight Board (PCAOB) standards
> Generally accepted government auditing standards
> Other standards

AICPA's Auditing Standards

The American Institute of Certified Public Accountants sets auditing standards for private companies, many nonprofit organizations, and some government entities. AICPA's Auditing Standards Board promulgates generally accepted auditing standards, including the Statements on Auditing Standards. Audit committee members do not need to be experts with these standards, but they should know the sources for these standards as applicable to their types of organizations.

PCAOB Standards

The Public Company Accounting Oversight Board sets the standards for audits of the financial statements of publicly traded companies. The Securities and Exchange Commission appoints the five members of the PCAOB and retains veto power over all of its proposed standards. As a result, the PCAOB is under the control of the SEC.

Generally Accepted Government Auditing Standards

The Government Accountability Office issues external auditing standards that apply to many government entities and some nonprofit organizations that receive government awards. These standards are referred to as generally accepted government auditing standards. In addition, the Government Accountability Office serves as the external auditor of the U.S. federal government, including the SEC.

Other Standards

While these three standard setters are the most influential in the United States, there are several others, most relating to government funding, such as the U.S. Department of Housing and Urban Development and the Office of Management and Budget. Although there are clearly differences between the auditing standards, they are all anchored in similar fundamentals pertaining to ethics, independence, auditors' professional judgment and competence, quality control, performance of the audit, and reporting. These are commonly referred to as general auditing standards. There are also numerous standards on the planning, fieldwork, and reporting aspects of the external audit process.

ACTION STEPS

▲ Know that your actions, or inactions, will be interpreted by the external auditors in assessing the effectiveness of the audit committee.

▲ Be vocal in raising questions, concerns, and expectations with the external auditor.

▲ Hold executive sessions with the external auditor that are closed to the CFO and any other managers or nonindependent directors.

Auditor Risk Standards

The implications of risk-assessment standards are significant. While the concept of risk has always been central to the audit process, these standards raise the bar in a number of areas, including financial statement disclosures (in footnotes, for example), consideration of fraud, and audit supervision. For example, the auditor is directed to increase its emphasis on consideration of potential management bias and risks related to missing or incomplete disclosures. There is also more emphasis on detecting fraud using fraud-driven procedures as an integral part of the entire audit process rather than as a discrete segment of the audit process. In addition, auditors and audit committee members alike should be on the lookout for misstatements related to revenue recognition, estimates, related-party transactions, and management and discussion analysis disclosures.

Open dialogue between audit committee members and the external auditor benefits both sides. Communication of significant risks identified by the auditor gives the audit committee an opportunity to understand the auditor's view of the risks of material misstatements. Likewise, the ability of the audit committee to provide an inside glimpse of the company to the auditor cannot be underestimated in terms of value to the auditor. It is an opportunity for the audit committee to point out risks that perhaps were previously unknown to the auditor.

Both the Auditing Standards Board and the PCAOB have a series of auditing standards collectively referred to as risk-assessment standards. These standards direct auditors to focus on a variety of risks at the heart of the audit process. They pertain to audit planning, supervision, materiality, assessing risk, responding to risk, and documenting risk.

One of the PCAOB risk-assessment standards, number 12, is especially worthy of a reading by audit committee members. It instructs the auditor to gain a solid grasp of the company's operating and control environments. This includes inquiries of the audit committee or its equivalent (or its chair), management, those performing the internal audit function, and others within the company who may reasonably be expected to have information that is important to the identification and assessment of risks of material misstatement.

PCAOB standard number 12 explicitly mentions the following inquiries that the auditor should make of the audit committee, its equivalent, or its chair regarding fraud risks:

1. The audit committee's views about fraud risks in the company

2. Whether the audit committee has knowledge of fraud, alleged fraud, or suspected fraud affecting the company

3. Whether the audit committee is aware of tips or complaints regarding the company's financial reporting (including those received through the audit committee's internal whistle-blower program, if such program exists) and, if so, the audit committee's responses to such tips and complaints

4. How the audit committee exercises oversight of the company's assessment of fraud risks and the establishment of controls to address fraud risks[5]

A risk-based approach to management and auditing is strongly encouraged because it helps with the alignment of resources where the greatest risks reside.

ACTION STEPS

▲ Don't rely solely on the external auditor to catch fraudulent acts and errors.

▲ Know that auditors consider your efforts to identify and assess risks of material misstatement.

▲ Address the topic of risk at every meeting, discussing identification, assessment, and management.

▲ Encourage lively debate between the auditor and the CFO.

▲ Promote two-way transparency with the auditor.

▲ Provide information on risk to auditors to improve the quality of the audit.

Potential Roles of the Auditor

The audit is most commonly associated with rendering an opinion on financial statements. Yet certified public accountant (CPA) firms offer a variety of services beyond the audit. Audit committees must remain cognizant of the dangers of stretching their auditor too far in terms of services, thus invoking either actual conflicts of interest or perceived conflicts of interest. Because auditors can perform additional services beyond the audit, audit committees should understand which other services their auditor can perform.

CPA firm services are broadly categorized as either assurance services or nonassurance services. Assurance services include audits, reviews, and agreed-upon procedures; nonassurance services include those services such as bookkeeping, tax preparation, and management consulting that have the CPA firm act in a quasi-management role. Examples of nonassurance services would include having the CPA firm design policies and procedures or perform transactions.

AICPA defines assurance services as independent professional services that improve the quality of information for decision makers. Generally, a CPA firm is prohibited for independence reasons from providing assurance services if it also provides nonassurance services to the same client. To avoid the use of the same CPA firm for both assurance and nonassurance services, it is generally best to avoid having the CPA performing audits and reviews also perform other services for the organization.

For an auditor to provide tax advice or vendor recommendation involves a closeness that can sound alarms regarding the auditor's independence. SOX lists nine explicitly prohibited service areas:

1. Bookkeeping or other services related to the accounting records or financial statements of the audit client
2. Financial information systems design and implementation
3. Appraisal or valuation services, fairness opinions, or contribution-in-kind reports

4. Actuarial services

5. Internal audit outsourcing services

6. Management functions or human resources

7. Broker or dealer, investment adviser, or investment banking services

8. Legal services and expert services unrelated to the audit

9. Any other service that the PCAOB determines is impermissible[6]

The SEC discusses each of these prohibited services in its final release, No. 33–8183. This release also defines the SEC's principles of independence with respect to services provided by auditors. It mentions the following three basic principles of auditor independence (violation of any one would impair the auditor's independence):

1. An auditor cannot function in the role of management.

2. An auditor cannot audit his or her own work.

3. An auditor cannot serve in an advocacy role for his or her client.[7]

The current audit-client environment is much different than prior to the Sarbanes-Oxley Act of 2002. For example, before SOX it was common for audit clients to ask their auditor to help draft footnotes to the financial statements or assist in the procurement of accounting software. Assisting in the preparation of the footnotes, which are integral to the financial statements, would put auditors in the position of auditing their own work. Regarding the example of advisory services of accounting software, this could impair the auditor's ability to objectively audit the numbers coming from the software since the auditor had a hand in the client's procuring it. These are important considerations and support the logic of having the audit committee preapprove all services performed by the auditor, since it is the audit committee members who are most likely in the best position to know the services and evaluate any lack of independence.

ACTION STEPS

▲ Avoid using the same CPA firm for both assurance and nonassurance services.

▲ Make sure that the audit committee approves all services performed by CPA firms to ensure that unintended conflicts between assurance and nonassurance services are avoided.

Hiring, Evaluating, and Replacing the External Auditor

Considering the importance of the audit function in helping to ensure the integrity of the financial statements, the audit committee needs to constantly monitor its relationship with the auditor. The committee needs to be prepared for the following situations regarding its external auditor:

> Finding a new auditor

> Evaluating the auditor annually

Finding a New Auditor

No one can predict when an auditor might resign or when a serious matter might arise where a discharge is in order. As a result, the audit committee must be prepared at all times with a contingency plan. This entails having a short list of two or three reliable audit firms that can be called upon. Audit committee members most likely have existing relationships with many CPA firms with whom they've done business or shared other business affiliations. However, audit committee members should be sensitive when receiving referrals from management to use a particular CPA firm because of the inherent conflict created when auditors evaluate the work of members of management for whom they owe their entrée into an organization. Especially concerning would be a recommendation from a manager to use a CPA firm that was a former employer, since the manager may still have colleagues there who could be susceptible to influence. Audit committees should also consider the firm's industry experience, size, geographical reach, and reputation, since these factors often serve as a proxy of quality for many readers of the financial statements.

There may even be a wish to change auditors as part of a forced auditor-rotation initiative. This is a topic about which many hold a strong opinion. On the one hand, changing auditors is costly, stressful, and sometimes awkward. There is a steep learning curve that must be climbed. On the other hand, auditor independence, objectivity, and professional skepticism tend to dissipate after many years on the job. Audit committee members should weigh these pros and cons in an effort to do what is best for their organization.

Then again, audit-firm rotation may soon be a requirement rather than an option because standard setters such as the PCAOB are looking at the concept of forced audit-firm rotation as a way to enhance independence, objectivity, and professional skepticism. For organizations looking at audit-firm rotation as a possibility, PCAOB Release number 2011–006, "Concept Release on Auditor Independence and Audit Firm Rotation" (August 16, 2011), is worth reading.

Evaluating the Auditor Annually

External auditors should be evaluated annually to ensure that the firm has retained the required independence and technical ability. The evaluation process needs to be led by the audit committee, but it is rarely done without input from the CFO, the chief audit executive (CAE), legal counsel, and others.

Audit committee members should be aware of typical biases of these roles. For example, management may be concerned that the auditor may evaluate management poorly; as a result, management may complain about it in an effort to get a different auditing team on board. Legal counsel may not like auditors who demand certain disclosure about commitments and contingent liabilities that attorneys consider to be confidential information prior to final resolution. Internal auditors may be defensive if they feel their work has been poorly viewed by the external auditor.

Factors that audit committees can use to evaluate an external auditor include:

> Auditor independence
> Technical ability
> Staff fatigue
> Audit fees

Auditor Independence

Because widespread acceptance of the audit report depends on the auditor's independence, audit committee members should consider both the external auditor's basic character (i.e., independence in fact) and the public's perception of whether the external auditor is independent (i.e., independence in appearance).

One measure of an auditor's independence is the level of candor in communications between the auditor and the audit committee. The lure of continued audit fees can be significant enough for some auditors to quash candid or, at times, adverse feedback. Auditors have tremendous insights into an organization's vulnerabilities, but they may shade the truth, even while complying with professional standards, in an effort to retain a client. Audit committee members must demand unvarnished truth, as this leads to a powerful source of value to the organization being audited. Committee members must communicate frequently with the audit partner, as this signals care and commitment to the audit process, as well as a desire to leverage the communication in an effort to take appropriate action.

Technical Ability

Auditors serve as a resource for audit committee members who may need counsel from time to time on technical matters. Therefore, audit committee members should be comfortable with the auditor's mastery of topics pertaining to risks and operating effectiveness, including:

> ➤ Entity-level controls, including "tone at the top"
> ➤ Automated controls, such as computerized tests that detect data-entry errors
> ➤ General information technology controls, such as user-name and password-enforced segregation of duties
> ➤ Antifraud controls, which can include the use of analytical procedures to detect fraud (see Chapter 9)

If the audit committee is not getting this information from its auditor, it may be time for a change.

Staff Fatigue

A common pet peeve of management is repeated requests from auditors for the same document. Another common management complaint is the frequent need to train new audit staff members, who seem to change every year as a result of the revolving-door style of staff assignments popular with many CPA firms. While these complaints are common to most audits, audit committees should be sensitive to undue fatigue for the organization's staff, as such practices may signal poor audit administration and supervision.

Audit Fees

While audit quality is foremost in the minds of the audit committee, auditor evaluation must include consideration of cost, such as hours billed for unproductive time, duplicative requests to the organization's staff, and bills for more expensive staff assigned to the audit than the work commands. In evaluating the audit fee quoted by an auditor, audit committees should consider opportunities to contain escalating audit fees by addressing the possibilities of unexpected expansions of scope, leveraging the internal audit function, and the need for assurance services on disclosures outside the financial statements.

Unexpected Expansions of Scope If the auditor feels uneasy about a certain account, estimate, class of transactions, finance-related department, etc., it expands the scope of the audit. Because the expansion of scope often leads to additional fees, there should be plenty of candid conversation between the audit committee and the auditor in the planning stage of the audit, including where the audit committee members see the most risk, so that the auditor can provide more accurate fee quotes. This approach runs contrary to the practice of some organizations that consider it an advantage to conceal high-risk areas.

Leveraging the Internal Audit Function If the organization has an internal audit function, audit committee members should advocate for the external auditor's ability to use the work of the internal auditor. Assuming the internal auditors are objective, competent, properly credentialed, and independent of the work they are assessing, the external auditor can reduce the procedures performed. The dividends to the organization can be significant, most notably through reduced external audit fees.

Need for Assurance Services on Disclosures Outside the Financial Statements All entities are subject to some degree of additional regulatory disclosures. These can range from tax returns to satisfying debt covenants to filing funding source reports to regulatory reporting, such as proxy statements, annual reports, and real-time reports as required by the SEC. Confirm the auditor's responsibilities for these disclosures and include the performance of the independent assurance activities in the original fee quote so that the performance of the auditor of these tasks is not added to the bill at the end of the audit.

ACTION STEPS

▲ Have contingency plans for replacing an auditor on short- and long-term time horizons.

▲ Challenge your external auditor by requesting information the committee can benefit from in fulfilling its duties.

▲ Exercise caution when filtering negative information received by management about the auditor.

CHAPTER FIVE

Scrutinize the Financial Statements

SO MUCH GOES ON within an organization at the operational level that it can be difficult to grasp its business reality just by reading board packets and listening to briefings from management. In this chapter, we focus on the common types of financial misstatements as well as on suggested governance protocols, discussing how directors can familiarize themselves with idiosyncratic back-office operations, including techniques to identify complex transactions that are more form than substance.

Types of Financial Misstatements

Headline-grabbing accounting scandals like Enron, which eroded shareholder value from $90 a share in August 2000 to less than a dollar in November 2001, illustrate the damaging effects of fraudulent financial misstatements. In hindsight, the egregious overstatement of revenues for Enron should have been easy to spot.

In their book *Financial Shenanigans*, Howard Schilit and Jeremy Perler noted that Enron increased revenue by a factor of 10 in just five years, reaching $100 billion in 2000. In 2000, only five other Fortune 500 companies had ever reached $100 billion in sales: ExxonMobil, Wal-Mart, General Motors, Ford Motor Company, and General

Electric. Schilit and Perler analyzed the years it took all six of these companies to go from $10 billion to $100 billion in sales, and Enron beat them all at just four years. Wal-Mart came in second at 10 years; ExxonMobil came in third at 17 years; and GM, Ford, and GE each took between 26 and 31 years to grow sales to this level.[1]

When Enron's growth is viewed by the short number of years it took for it to break the $100 billion mark, its downfall seems to have been inevitable when one considers Enron's business model, which did not appear to generate economic growth. Yet its meteoric growth was assumed to be supported by a new business model that could sustain such economic growth. What audit committee members and board directors can gather from the Enron scandal is that year-on-year growth should be closely scrutinized and that too-good-to-be-true growth is most likely unsustainable regardless of management's explanations.

As a counterpoint, another company, Apple, has exceeded sales of $100 billion since Schilit's and Perler's analysis of organizations exceeding $100 billion in sales as of 2000. Apple grew from a $10 billion to a $100 billion company in just seven years, from 2004 to 2011. Apple's business model of creating and marketing stylish, affordable, must-have electronic devices makes a solid case for authentic generation of wealth. In contrast to Enron, Apple's growth can be easily understood.

Accurate financial reporting serves as the cornerstone of board oversight, arming directors with data points that ensure that the organization is meeting agreed-upon goals and providing early warning signs of impending disaster. Yet motivations abound for senior managers to distort financial information, especially when those distortions allow managers to enhance their personal wealth through incentives and bonuses. Some managers are lured into distorting financial reporting to improve personal or organizational prestige. Still more managers distort the financial picture as a desperate act to stay in business. Directors need to be aware that the incentive is not always to overstate earnings. At times, understating income may be done for tax advantages. Typical financial misstatements fall into the broad categories of revenue misstatements, expense misstatements, inflated assets, and misleading disclosures.

Revenue Misstatements

The leading source of financial statement fraud shows up as overstated earnings. Accounting and Auditing Enforcement Releases from the SEC from 1982 through 2005 indicate that 52.8 percent of misstatements are attributed to revenue-recognition issues. There are several varieties of revenue-recognition fraud schemes, all of which involve an organization claiming income in the current period for the delivery of goods or services that were not performed. Such manipulation may involve recording sales for nonexistent services, as was the case with ZZZZ Best in the 1980s, in which founder Barry Minkow reported income for nonexistent services.

Now an infamous example of fraud, ZZZZ Best went public in December 1986, eventually earning a market capitalization of more than $200 million. It was launched as a carpet cleaning company, but Minkow eventually branched out into insurance restoration contracts. The problem was, the firm was little more than an elaborate Ponzi scheme. Barely a year later, the firm collapsed, costing stakeholders more than $100 million, the largest accounting fraud in history at the time.

Revenue misstatement may also result from front-loading sales from future periods, which is taking legitimate sales and recording them before the goods or services are completely delivered. Front-loading sales can take two forms, one in which the sales are recorded prematurely as a matter of record keeping, as was the case with Computer Associates. The firm booked $1.8 billion of fiscal year 2000 sales in 1999, nearly a third of its revenue. Computer Associates later restated a combined $2.2 billion in sales that it booked improperly in both 1999 and 2000.[2]

Recording sales prematurely by shipping goods ahead of customer-specified preferences, also known as channel-stuffing, also is an easy path for fraud. Florafax International restated 1998 earnings, taking reported earnings from $1.768 million to a loss of $623,000.

The correction reversed sales for goods shipped without customer authorization.[3] Revenue misstatement also frequently involves the manipulation of receivables when organizations take an overly optimistic position on the collectibility of past-due accounts and understate the allowance for doubtful debts.[4]

Expense Misstatements

Misstating expenses is another common way of distorting financial information. Accounting standards allow for purchases to be recorded as an asset if there is a benefit to future periods. Expense misstatements would involve recording a purchase that is consumed in the current period as an asset rather than an expense. For example, in the case of WorldCom, the company's own internal audit department determined that senior managers had used aggressive capitalization of expenses to hide $3.8 billion in expenses.[5] WorldCom had for years been suspected of using questionable accounting methods to hide its declining financial condition in hopes of increasing its stock price. It was found that WorldCom's total assets had been inflated by approximately $11 billion. In 2002, WorldCom filed for Chapter 11 bankruptcy, the largest such filing in U.S. history at the time.

Capitalization of expenses is a well-regarded accounting principle that allows for matching the timing of the recognition of expenses with the period the benefit is realized. So, if an organization buys something in year one that will be of benefit for five years, organizations are likely to capitalize the expense as an asset and then recognize one-fifth of the expense in each of the five years. The problem with WorldCom was that routine expenses were capitalized without clear logic that future periods would benefit from current expenses. Such aggressive capitalization of expenses allowed WorldCom to understate current expenses, thereby improving reported earnings and increasing reported assets.

In a survey of financial misstatements reported in the Accounting and Auditing Enforcement Releases from the SEC from 1982 through 2005, capitalizing expenses by creating an asset from a purchase instead of properly recording a purchase as an expense of the current period occurred approximately 27.2 percent of the time. Additional expense-related misstatements were attributed to manipulations of costs of goods sold and inventory (11.4 percent and 132 percent, respectively), which can occur when management loads inventory costs with nonmanufacturing expenses when imputing manufacturing-overhead charges.[6]

Inflated Assets

As stated earlier, categorizing purchases as an asset with benefits to future periods instead of an expense of the current period can inflate the value of assets. Management can also inflate assets by understating reserves recorded against inventory, receivables, and fixed assets. Reserves for inventory (obsolescence), accounts receivable (doubtful accounts), and fixed assets (permanent impairment) are designed to allow managers to reduce the reported value of assets when the value of said assets has decreased. Managers can use the easing and tightening of such reserves as a "cookie jar" to smooth earnings by tweaking the percentage reserved incrementally to achieve desired earnings targets. "Cookie jar accounting" is a misleading practice used to smooth income by using reserves from good years to offset losses from bad years.

In 2009, for example, the SEC fined General Electric $50 million for utilizing cookie jar accounting and other questionable methods to smooth earnings. GE was said to have falsified $995 million in sales during 2002 and 2003, which helped bump up its stock price and double the company's market capitalization.

Inventory amounts can be overstated when management underestimates losses associated with obsolete inventory. Audit committee members can review slow-and-no-moving inventory figures as well as number-of-days-sales-in-inventory figures to identify anomalies between reported reserves for obsolescence and likely obsolescence amounts.

Accounts receivable can be manipulated when earnings are declared prematurely, thus increasing the amounts reported as due from customers. In addition, management can understate the reserve for doubtful accounts to improve reported accounts-receivable amounts. Audit committee and board members can evaluate the adequacy of accounts-receivable reserves by considering collectibility of balances due for invoices aged over 90 days, historical bad debt expense, and delinquency rates by customer. Be aware, though, that when credit policies become more lax, historical customer-collection rates may be better than expected collections for sales to customers who qualified under looser credit standards. (A more detailed discussion of manipulation of inventory obsolescence and accounts receivable reserves appears in the sections "Accounts Receivables" and "Inventory" under "The Role of Management Estimates" later in this chapter.)

Fixed assets can also be overstated in instances where market values of properties are permanently depressed. Accounting principles allow for organizations to account for assets purchased on a cost basis, meaning fixed assets are valued at an amount equal to what an organization paid. However, accounting principles dictate that organizations must write down the value of fixed assets (and certain investments as well) if the market value of the property declines significantly from the amount paid when such declines are believed to be permanent. Such a reduction in the value of fixed assets, and in certain investment categories, is described as the permanent impairment of assets. Recent economic conditions suggest that many real estate holdings, for example, are permanently depressed. Therefore, audit committee members and board directors should discuss in earnest with management the possibility that fixed assets are overstated.

Misleading Disclosures

Footnotes to financial statements are an integral part of external reporting, clarifying such important matters as selection of accounting policies, contingent liabilities, and reporting at the segment level. Management selection of accounting policies can swing income and net asset numbers significantly based on the organization's policies on when revenues and expenses are recognized. Organizations that recognize revenues early and expenses late can distort the financial position of the organization that is reported to third parties.

Contingent liabilities alert readers to possible charges to the organization in future periods. These liabilities can include matters related to legal or regulatory uncertainty. In cases where footnotes are misleading, omissions of contingent liabilities are far more common than false statements. Research by Hollis Skaife and Daniel Wangerin indicates that a leading factor for failed merger and acquisition activity is improper accounting for leases, contingencies, and off-balance sheet liabilities. The research warned that "having to book these additional liabilities as a result of completing the deal could trigger debt covenant violations for the acquiring firms."[7]

Segment-level reporting offers additional opportunities to distort financial reporting when reporting segments based on geographic, product, or customer market are chosen to conceal unprofitable areas by netting the performance of underperforming segments with segments showing strong performance results. For example, a sporting goods company can report at the segment level geographically, state-to-state, or domestic-or-global sales, or by customer (e.g., women versus men). Now imagine that women's sales are underperforming. Management could conceal that by reporting sales as either domestic or international and avoid reporting based on customer type altogether. Only publicly traded entities are required to disclose a change such as this in segment-level reporting.

In trying to evaluate the quality of financial statement footnote disclosures, research has considered the readability of the footnotes. One of the measures of the readability of the English language is called the Gunning Fog Index. Calculation of the Gunning Fog Index is based on an algorithm that considers the average length of the sentence and frequency of complex words. A Gunning Fog Index calculator is available at http://gunning-fog-index.com.

The index works best for passages of about 100 words. Passages that receive a Gunning Fog Index of at least 8 are considered to be universally understood. Passages that receive a Fog Index of 12 are assumed to be readable to audiences with a reading level of a high school senior (i.e., a 12th grader). The Gunning Fog Index of the footnotes for many publicly traded companies' financial reports for 2011 fell within the 15–20 range. A Gunning Fog Index of 15–20 suggests that the wording is easily absorbed by those with at least

15–20 years of education. For comparison purposes, Microsoft's disclosure of its revenue-recognition policy in 2011 was 21, and Best Buy's disclosure of its contingencies in 2011 was 14. As evidence of the linkage between complex footnotes and possible financial statement fraud, Gemstar TV Guide received a Gunning Fog Index of 38 for its 2001 disclosure of contingent revenue, indicating a readership level of 38 years of education. The SEC charged Gemstar's former CEO and CFO in 2003 for "their roles in the widespread and complex scheme to inflate Gemstar's licensing and advertising revenues."[8]

Additional research on the link between misleading disclosures and financial statement fraud was reported by the American Accounting Association in 2010. In the report *Can Linguistic Predictors Detect Fraudulent Financial Filings?*, researchers delved into quantifying the connection between fraud and misleading disclosures using two dimensions that indicated fraud: number of words per sentence and number of sentences per paragraph. The researchers reported that fraudulent 10-K filings averaged 31 words per sentence, while nonfraudulent financial statements averaged 17. Furthermore, fraudulent filings averaged four sentences per paragraph, while nonfraudulent 10-K filings averaged about two.[9]

The researchers also identified several words as being effective in predicting and detecting fraud. Among them were *weaknesses, conclusions, qualitative, quantitative, summarize, purported, cooperating, aggregate,* and *counterparties*.[10] Audit committees should exercise additional caution and perhaps inquire more deeply on the underlying business activity for footnotes with common use of these words or for documents with a poor Gunning Fog Index.

ACTION STEPS

▲ Focus on the common types of financial misstatements: overstated revenues, understated expenses, inflated assets, and misleading disclosures.

▲ Evaluate the likelihood of misleading disclosures based on the readability of the writing.

▲ Ensure that footnotes are clear, readable, and of high quality.

Governance Protocols

Board directors and audit committee members can rely on a variety of governance protocols to help identify financial misstatements, including addressing the expectation gap, assessing the culture over financial reporting, and utilizing tools to scrutinize financial data presented.

Addressing the Expectation Gap

The expectation gap refers to the perceived deficiencies between what audited financial statements are and what the public thinks they are. With so many high-profile accounting frauds perpetrated under the nose of some of the largest CPA firms, stakeholders have been left to wonder just what an audit does. Understanding the limitations of the external audit allows audit committee members to fill in the expectation gap with additional procedures, performed either by a member of the audit committee or by a designated representative such as a certified public accountant or a fraud examiner.

Myths about audits abound and include the misperceptions that audits are designed to detect fraud; that the auditors, not management, are responsible for the financial statements; that clean audit opinions imply that the data reported are precise; and that auditors are capable of warning investors of impending business failure. It is management that must take responsibility for the financial statements. Although auditors often prepare or assist in preparing financial statements, management alone is accountable for their contents.

To address the expectation gap, audit committee members should understand the role of materiality, sampling, selection of accounting policies, and auditor communications in the audit process.

Materiality

Materiality is an accounting convention whereby auditors make a determination of the importance readers place on the size of an error. Errors deemed immaterial can be waived without adjusting the company's financial statements, whereas auditors require material errors to be corrected before issuing a clean audit opinion. The difficulty with auditors' determining what is material and what is immaterial is that the sensitivity of the readers of these financial statements may vary widely. Readers with greater sensitivity to errors can be disappointed by the size of errors that auditors allow to go uncorrected.

Readers of financial statements should know that a quantitative standard has not emerged, leaving a great deal of discretion to the auditors in determining materiality. Typical measures used in determining materiality can include, but are not limited to, using percentages of net income (perhaps 5 percent errors), total assets (possibly 1 percent error in valuing total assets), total revenue (perhaps 1 percent error), and equity (possibly 1 percent error).

In reviewing the range of materiality amounts with calculations based on Microsoft's 2011 public filing (see Figure 5.1), for example, it is apparent that auditors have a wide range when determining materiality, making meeting the needs and interests of all readers of the financial statements difficult. Under the guidelines listed above, the materiality for Microsoft could be deemed professionally appropriate with an error range that starts as low as approximately $570,000 and goes up to nearly $700 million. Given such a wide range of tolerable materiality amounts allowed by the profession, audit committee members should communicate openly with both internal and external auditors to ensure that the materiality limits applied conform to expectations.

Account	%	2011 Amount	Materiality
Total revenue	1%	$69,943,000,000	$699,430,000
Net income	5%	23,150,000	1,157,500
Total assets	1%	108,704,000	1,087,040
Equity	1%	57,083,000	570,830

Figure 5.1   Possible calculation of materiality for Microsoft, based on amounts reported in 2011 10-K.

Sampling

While most stakeholders do not expect external auditors to test 100 percent of the data, some readers of the financial statements, which may include creditors or regulators, may expect that auditors test more of the data than they actually do. In most cases, internal auditors test more of the data than external auditors do. Even so, readers of financial statements should be aware that sampling is applied liberally in the audit process and that, therefore, the possibility exists that unknown errors are present. Thus stakeholders should be aware that not all values reported are based on 100 percent verification and that errors may occur in those accounts that lend themselves well to test sampling.

Selection of Accounting Policies

Readers of financial statements should be mindful of the role of accounting policies in the way financial information is presented. Two of the more fundamental principles of accounting that influence the manner in which financial information is reported are linked to the concepts of conservatism and matching.

Conservatism in accounting directs auditors to report assets at historical cost, i.e., the amount paid for an asset. In using historical cost, appreciated assets do not increase the total assets reported. In a departure from cost-basis accounting, certain assets are marked-to-market (e.g., marketable securities held for sale). In addition, auditors may mark down assets if the devaluation is deemed to be permanent, with such a condition described as a permanent impairment of an asset.

Subsequent recovery of lost value of devalued assets cannot be later written up. The lowest valuation would stand until the asset is sold. Conservatism should provide helpful insight to readers of financial statements because overvaluation of assets would be more injurious than undervaluation. Even so, readers should be aware that asset valuations may not reflect the current economic status of an organization or its liquidation value.

The matching principle instructs accountants to capitalize the cost of assets that have a benefit to future periods rather than expensing the full cost of an asset in the year of purchase. Once an asset is capitalized, it will be depreciated over its useful life. A piece of equipment that costs $100,000 and has an estimated useful life of 10 years may show up in the income statement at a cost of $10,000 per year for 10 years rather than $100,000 in year one. The matching principle satisfies the interests of readers because if an organization were allowed to record an expense of $100,000 in year one and no expenses for the remaining nine years the asset is in use, the organization would look horrible in year one but look great for the remaining nine years. While the matching principle is largely a benefit to readers, all stakeholders should be mindful of the effects of this matching because depreciation methods smooth earnings and may not reflect the remaining value of the equipment if the asset had to be sold immediately.

In addition to the principles of conservatism and matching that apply to all organizations, managers make other decisions that can affect the presentation of financial information. These include revenue-recognition decisions and capitalization policies that affect the period in which revenues and expenses are recorded. Readers should be aware that while the accounting policies adopted may conform with generally accepted accounting principles, all accounting methods have limitations that can create clumsy outcomes on the balance sheet and income statements.

For example, with straight-line depreciation, in which the value of the asset is expensed evenly over all the years of an asset's useful life, the reality is that the actual value of the asset does not decline evenly over all years. In most cases, the market value of the asset declines significantly more in the early years of the asset's life. Furthermore, straight-line depreciation assumes even usage in all years, which may not be the case. However, because some method of depreciation must be used, imperfect methods are sometimes applied for expediency and consistency. Readers should be aware that as long as organizations adopt accounting policies in conformance with GAAP and those policies are applied consistently, auditors are likely to allow financial information to be reported in a way that may not meet the expectation of all readers.

Auditor Communications

Even auditors who provide a clean audit opinion can utilize other communication to express important information that can do much to reduce the expectation gap for those readers such as audit committees, lenders, and regulators who have the right to ask for information not available to the general public. Other methods of communication include the schedule of uncorrected errors, management letter comments, the management representation letter, and even the audit report date.

Schedule of Uncorrected Errors As part of the audit, auditors use a schedule of uncorrected errors to record those differences deemed immaterial. Audit committee members can request access to this list. As mentioned in the discussion about materiality, what the auditor deems immaterial may in fact be material to certain readers. In addition, even immaterial differences should not be ignored, because some may point to dysfunctional processes that could cause business failure or serve as a red flag for fraud. Although most third parties cannot access the schedule of uncorrected errors because of confidentiality customs of private organizations and existing shareholder rights designed to reduce voluminous records requests by third parties for publicly traded companies, audit committee members can and should be particularly attentive to items that appear on the schedule of uncorrected errors. The items listed as uncorrected errors signal to audit committees areas of concern that could point to a control deficiency or fraud.

Management Letter Comments Management letters typically list control weaknesses noted during the audit. For publicly traded companies in the Sarbanes-Oxley era, material control weaknesses must be reported in public filings. The pressure of reporting these weaknesses has prompted most organizations that publicly file to correct any noted weaknesses. As a result, many publicly traded organizations report no material weaknesses at their fiscal year end since the deficiencies have already been remediated.

For other organizations, management letter comments can provide insights into control weaknesses that could impact future periods if not corrected. The quality of the information available in management letter comments varies widely based on the writing skill and candor of the auditor. Some auditors stick to boilerplate comments that give away little about the inner workings of the organization, while other auditors carefully craft comments designed to promote adoption of recommendations. For example, the auditor may simply state that the organization should improve segregation of duties. Such a broad recommendation is not as helpful as the suggestion by an auditor that the same accounts receivable clerk should not both approve credit memos and post customer payments. Such an arrangement would allow for the same person to pocket customer payments and adjust the customer account with a credit memo to indicate no balance due.

Audit committee members should review management letter comments closely in the hope that the auditor reveals limitations in the organization's controls and processes. In the event that a company's external auditor does not provide management letter comments, the audit committee should inquire why and ask the auditor for verbal comments about controls.

Management Representation Letter The writing of a management representation letter is a standard procedure completed before the auditor signs the audit report. The management letter is ostensibly written by management to the auditor and states, among other things, that the information presented to the auditor is accurate to the best of management's knowledge. In practice, however, the management letter is often prepared by the auditor, printed on the client's letterhead, and then signed by senior members of management, such as the CEO and CFO.

In drafting the management letter, the auditor typically begins with language indicated by auditing standards. If there were areas of the audit in which the auditor relied heavily on the representations of management, those specific assertions get added to the end of the list of standard management letter representations. Audit committee members should be particularly attentive to those assertions, as they point to elements of the audit for which the auditor could have been unable to verify management assertions with third-party information; thus, the items listed in the management representation letter may suggest that some elements of the audit are more susceptible to management manipulation.

Audit Report Date The audit report date may give away no special information, especially if the report date falls within 90 days of the balance sheet date. However, for those report dates that fall beyond the 90-day mark, such a late report date may indicate that the organization faced a going-concern issue.

A going-concern issue arises when the auditor has doubts that the organization will stay in business 12 months after the balance sheet date, with only those organizations free of a going-concern issue receiving the much-coveted clean opinion. Because most organizations would rather wait for a clean opinion, auditors may delay issuing a report until the going-concern issue has been resolved.

The going-concern issue may be resolved either through the organization receiving a pledge from an investor to fund any operating losses through the 12-month period or through the passage of time. Organizations with a going-concern issue have received clean opinions with report dates as late as November or December into the following year for organizations with a December 31 year-end. Some organizations have waited and reported two years at once to avoid getting a going-concern opinion. While the report date may mean nothing, audit committee members should be suspicious of the organization's financial sustainability if the report is issued beyond 90 days of the balance sheet date.

ACTION STEPS

▲ Address the expectation gap by considering the effects of:

   ◑ Auditor's assessment of materiality

   ◑ Management's selection of accounting policies

▲ Spot early signs of trouble by looking for auditor's insights revealed in the:

   ◑ Schedule of uncorrected errors

   ◑ Management letter comments

   ◑ Management representation letter

   ◑ Audit report date

Assessing the Culture over Financial Reporting

Assessing the culture over financial reporting is a qualitative assessment that informs the level of scrutiny, for good or bad, that board directors and audit committee members must bring to bear when evaluating financial information presented by management. Key factors to consider in assessing the culture over financial reporting include the presence of an effective internal auditing staff; the performance of annual external audits; the integrity of decision makers involved in estimating financial statement values; the willingness of management to post significant adjustments or adverse disclosures; and the incentives, pressures, and opportunities to commit financial statement fraud.

Presence of an Effective Internal Auditing Staff

As noted, having an effective internal audit staff supports the goals of the audit committee by identifying control weakness in both design and execution, with positive results improving director confidence and poor results signaling a higher probability of misleading financial statements. The benefits of having an internal audit function are that external auditors can rely on the work of internal auditors and there is a lower likelihood of misstatements because of the in-house oversight provided by internal auditors.

Performance of Annual External Audits

Although external audits are not designed to identify fraud and have one of the lower fraud-detection rates among the prevailing fraud-deterrence tools, having an external audit performed, regardless of the existence of the internal audit function, provides assurance to board directors and audit committee members that the accounting principles selected by management are sound and that those accounting policies were applied consistently. The assurance of having an external audit performed lends credibility to the financial information reported. The lack of an external audit places more pressure on board directors and audit committee members to evaluate for themselves the soundness of accounting policies selected. It also creates a need to verify that those accounting policies selected were applied uniformly.

Integrity of Decision Makers Involved in Estimating Financial Statement Values

Some of the areas of financial reports most susceptible to fraud are those accounts that require estimates for losses. Such accounts include the accounts receivable allowance for bad debt, inventory's reserve for obsolescence, and fixed asset and investment impairment. For banks, for example, loan loss reserves require a great deal of judgment by management. Therefore, the integrity of decision makers involved in estimating financial statement values, which may only be judged by seeing how managers respond to morally complex challenges, is critical in evaluating the soundness of the financial statements. Experience may be the best predictor of integrity, with managers who have in the past pushed the ethical limits in compliance matters posing the greatest threat to sound judgments in estimating financial statement values. Managers who rely on "supportable positions" in tax, which is to say defensible tax positions that are favorable to an aggressive degree, and other compliance matters may be more likely to underreserve for losses to asset accounts and, therefore, are worthy of a higher level of scrutiny by the audit committee.

Willingness of Management to Post Significant Adjustments or Adverse Disclosures

As with the case of the integrity of decision makers in estimating financial statement values, the integrity of managers also influences the likelihood that management posts adjustments suggested by the auditors. Auditors may not require all proposed adjustments to be posted, because the effect of not posting the adjustment would be immaterial to the reader of the financial statements. But having managers who post only corrections forced upon them by auditors would indicate that other decisions made by management are aggressive and may not reflect the intentions of the board. Discussions with auditors to assess the willingness or unwillingness of management to post significant adjustments or adverse disclosures helps board directors and audit committee members assess the culture over financial reporting.

It also would be productive for audit committee members to solicit information about any accounting treatments that were heavily negotiated with management, as knowledge of such highly contested topics could serve as a guide for future discussions the audit committee members may choose to have among themselves and with management and auditors to ensure that the final resolution was appropriate.

Incentives, Pressures, and Opportunities to Commit Financial Statement Fraud

Incentives, pressures, and opportunities to commit financial statement fraud erode the culture over financial reporting. Therefore, it is important for audit committees and board directors to think about these elements when considering the likelihood of fraudulent misstatements.

Incentives Incentives for financial statement fraud typically include direct economic interests in the form of executive compensation and increased shareholder value. However, incentives for financial statement fraud can develop any time that individual interests, such as reputational gains or other nonmonetary rewards, are tied to organizational performance.

Three studies have examined the role of performance-based executive-compensation arrangements and the likelihood of financial misstatements. In the research paper "Executive Option Exercises and Financial Misreporting," Natasha Burns and Simi Kedia concluded that executives of firms that "deliberately adopted aggressive accounting practices exercised significantly more options in the misreported years in comparison to non-restating firms . . . [and had] much higher incidence of the opportunistic use of private information."[11]

In another research paper, "CEO Incentives and Earnings Management," Daniel Bergstresser and Thomas Philippon presented "evidence that more 'incentivized' CEOs—those whose overall compensation is more sensitive to company share prices—lead companies with higher levels of earnings management . . . [with] periods of high accruals coinciding with unusually significant option exercises by CEOs and unloading of shares by CEOs and other top executives."[12]

And in "Is There a Link Between Executive Compensation and Accounting Fraud?" Merle Erickson, Michelle Hanlon, and Edward Maydew find that the likelihood of accounting fraud increases in direct proportion to the percentage of total executive compensation that is stock-based.

These findings, along with related research, indicate that audit committees of organizations that include a performance-based compensation component for management must be aware of the increased fraud risk inherent in performance-based pay structures and they must scrutinize financial results that benefit management with increased skepticism.

Researchers are also aware, however, of the advantages of aligning executive interests with organizational gains, with Erickson et al. concluding that audit committees and compensation committees alike can appreciate that "a trade-off [exists] between the positive incentive effects afforded by performance-based compensation and the negative side effects, such as increasing the probability of accounting fraud."[13]

Pressures While incentives for personal gain can prompt managers to misstate financial information, the threat of a negative outcome can also put pressure on managers to provide misleading financial information. While audit committee members do not have a direct role in alleviating pressures, they should nonetheless remain cognizant that they exist. Such pressures can include unrealistic productivity expectations and earnings targets, financial losses if organizational indebtedness is tied to personal guarantees of owners and senior executives, and the need to meet third-party expectations.

Third-party expectations can include earnings goals expected on Wall Street or the satisfaction of loan covenants provided by lenders. The presence of recurring negative cash flows, operating losses, increased competitive pressures, and impending product obsolescence all increase the likelihood that managers may be susceptible to pressure to falsify financial statements.

Opportunities Once audit committee members and board members are attuned to the higher risk associated with the incentives and pressures to commit financial statement fraud, the opportunities to commit such fraud must be evaluated to understand the likelihood of the organization publishing misleading financial statements.

Critical elements for audit committee members to consider in evaluating the opportunities to commit financial statement fraud include the domination of management by one person or a small group, the presence of related-party transactions, the prevalence of highly complex transactions, and the existence of an overly complex organizational structure.

The domination of management by one person or a small group can make it easy for managers to manipulate financial results. Domination by one person or a small group may have broader implications that extend beyond the accuracy of financial reporting because the domination of one voice in an executive session, for example, can skew the decision-making abilities of the group in strategic and operational arenas as well.

Related-party transactions also pose fraud risk, though these transactions can be managed effectively as long as they are disclosed and independently evaluated to ensure arms-length terms have been met. The larger risk with such transactions is when they are unreported. (Tips for addressing unreported related-party transactions are discussed in Chapter 9 and include the use of a whistle-blower hotline and lifestyle audits.)

The prevalence of highly complex transactions increases the fraud risk of misleading statements because the added complexity makes it easier for managers to employ aggressive accounting procedures while evading the scrutiny of watchdogs. Audit committee members and board members should be on the alert for highly complex transactions in which the fundamentals of how genuine economic growth is generated seem unclear. For example, a Big Four auditing firm in the Midwest advised one of its clients to avoid dealing with Enron as a trade counterparty because the firm could not understand how Enron's meteoric growth was supported by genuine economic growth. This was smart advice, but in practice it can be hard for some committee members to ask too many questions regarding the soundness of a business model for fear that needing an explanation or clarification of a business model implies a lack of business acumen.

This inhibition is shared by many successful businesspeople. Audit committee members must not be afraid to ask the basic questions of how new, seemingly profitable deals make money. Nor can they stop inquiries when faced by resistance intended to silence them. Audit committee members should be especially wary if explanations include statements such as, "There are nuances to this that you don't understand." This is nonsense, because almost any plan for economic growth can be explained. When encountering complex transactions that have no ready explanation, it is likely that the transaction is more form than substance.

Concerns about overly complex organizational structures with regard to misleading financial information stem from opportunities such structures provide managers to combine the ill effects of related-party transactions and highly complex transactions. In the Enron case, CFO Andrew Fastow "created hundreds of 'special-purpose entities' designed to transfer Enron's debt to an outside company and get it off the books—without giving up control of the assets that stood behind the debt."[14]

While many audit committee members and board directors are unlikely to encounter the overly complex organizational structures seen with the Enron scandal, complex organizational structures could still pose a threat to accurate financial statements. Organizations that have subsidiaries that are not consolidated or trade partners with common ownerships should be particularly vigilant.

ACTION STEPS

▲ Evaluate the likelihood of misleading financial statements based on the integrity of managers, including their willingness to make significant adjustments or adverse disclosures.

▲ Consider the incentives to commit financial statement fraud inherent to performance-based executive compensation arrangements.

▲ Be cautious of the pressures for managers to provide misleading financial statements based on the need to protect personal economic interests where organizational debt is secured by personal guarantees.

▲ Know that third-party expectations of analysts and lenders influence the pressure managers feel to provide misleading financial information.

▲ Be aware of the opportunities that abound to commit financial statement fraud, including the domination of management by one person or a small group, the presence of related-party transactions, the prevalence of highly complex transactions, and the existence of an overly complex organizational structure.

Utilizing Tools to Scrutinize Financial Information Presented

Oversight of the financial information presented acts as the basis of the audit committee function. The challenge for board members lies in identifying tools to scrutinize financial information prepared by management. To sniff out errors, intentional or otherwise, the audit committee should focus on identifying key performance indicators to watch as well as the role of management estimates.

Key Performance Indicators to Watch

First and foremost, audit committee members and board members need to be cognizant of what is set before them with regard to financial information. It is the finance group that designs the board packet, determining which key performance indicators are tracked and analyzed. There are significant limitations in most board packets, with content often being too much or too little. Too little information makes it impossible for audit committee members to render educated judgments. Too much information makes it difficult to focus on the truly important information. Information that could serve as a red flag of impending doom could be buried in too much data to be useful.

Audit committee members can be exposed to liability because they should have acted on a problem but didn't. Audit committees and board directors must insist on meaningful reporting. For organizations that require copious data in board packets, effort should be made to offer a summary to the report.

Another consideration with financial reporting to boards is not just which key performance indicators to report but also at what level of detail, and board members should know that management can distort the way financial information is reported based on the way segments are categorized (e.g., geographic or by business unit, product line, or manager). For example, we worked with an organization with an operating budget of $1 million that had suffered losses of almost $2 million over a 10-year period without notice by the board because of the way the financial results were grouped. In this case, one manager was culpable for the entire loss, but the financial information presented to the board was segmented by geographic region rather than by manager. Had the board been reviewing financial performance by manager, the source of the problem would have been quite evident. Instead, the organization limped along for years. While reporting by manager rather than geography may not be the key to all organizations, thought should be given to which segment categories are used as key performance indicators, especially when there are unexplained losses at the entity level.

Lastly, board members need to be bold in verifying management explanations for unexpected results with third parties. For example, if management justifies a worsening gross margin by saying that cost of sales went up, whether it be from increasing raw material prices or the need to find a new supplier, the board is certainly within its rights to speak to the purchasing manager, especially if the jump in cost of sales is significant.

Further gains in the quality of information reported to the board, as evidenced by both the selection of key performance indicators and segment-level reporting, can be had when board members consider which financial and nonfinancial metrics they would like to see in the board packet.

Financial Metrics The choice of which financial metrics to include in the board packet depends largely on the size of the organization, ownership structure, industry, and specific risk profile. Some financial metrics to watch for early signs of trouble include gross margin, sales growth, cash flows from operations, and working capital.

> **Gross Margin** Gross margin and its components—revenue and cost of sales—are metrics tracked almost universally. Board members must be skeptical of even small changes in gross margin. They also should look for unusual relationships between recorded sales volume and production statistics, in that these two metrics typically move together. Additional skepticism should be applied

when, for example, sales volume growth exceeds production increases.

Unfortunately for Koss Corp., a Wisconsin-based designer and manufacturer of headphones, board members were not attentive enough to the downward trend in gross margins as an embezzlement scheme was under way that ended up costing shareholders more than $30 million. As noted in Figure 5.2, Koss experienced a decrease in revenue, as did many organizations shortly after the crash in autumn 2008.

What is notable in the financial information presented is that the cost of sales did not decrease proportionately with the declining sales. There could have been plausible explanations, including the presence of long-term supplier contracts, that kept costs stagnant while prices dropped. While it may never be publicly known what was discussed in the boardroom at Koss concerning the cause of the worsening gross margins prior to the discovery of the fraud, it is notable that these financial results were known by all including the board months before the fraud was discovered. Insiders never picked up on the fraud scheme. The fraud was discovered by a third party, American Express, which contacted Koss out of concern that the embezzler's personal charge account was being paid by a company wire transfer.

Koss Corp.
Financial Statements

	2006	2007	2008	2009
Revenues	$51	$46	$47	$38
Cost of Sales	31	28	29	25
Gross Margin	20	18	18	13
Gross Profit Percentage	39%	39%	38%	35%

(Currency stated in millions)

Figure 5.2 Koss Corp. financial results, 2006–2009.
Source: Form 10-K filing

Apparently, those charged with governance inside the company were unable to make use of what could have been an early sign of trouble.

Sales Growth Sales growth is usually a good thing. However, for organizations that are posting rapid growth, deceptive revenue-recognition schemes could be at play. Audit committee members should look closely at year-on-year growth statistics, especially if the organization's growth outpaces the growth of the industry overall.

Cash Flows from Operations Cash flows from operations, as reported on the statement of cash flows, should trend in a similar fashion as net income numbers. It would be odd for an organization to post significant earnings while reporting large negative cash flows from operations, with such a condition suggesting a possible fraudulent scheme.

Working Capital Working capital provides a snapshot of an organization's ability to meet current obligations. It is calculated by subtracting current liabilities from current assets. Some organizations operate with positive equity but with large short-term liabilities backed by long-term, possibly illiquid assets. Audit committee members should be mindful of watching the working capital to be sure that there is not a mismatch of risk inherent to having its long-term assets backed by short-term liabilities, as was the case with Lehman Brothers before its collapse.

Nonfinancial Metrics Financial metrics, while serving as the backbone of many board packets, are just one way of reviewing the inner workings of an organization. Nonfinancial metrics can alert audit committees and board members to trouble concealed by management. For example, customer returns and production reworks can alert the board to quality problems. A review of repeat customers can help quantify customer satisfaction, while tracking growth of new customers can help support the reason behind recent revenue growth.

Board members and audit committee members should periodically review the composition of the organization's top vendors and customers. The list of top five customers and vendors doesn't change very often, so there should not be any big surprise from year to year on the composition of the list. Still, it can be informative to see if the share of business among the top vendors and customers has changed significantly. For instance, if a vendor has typically enjoyed 30 percent of the organization's purchases and then gets 60 or 70 percent of the purchases, this could suggest a fraudulent relationship between the purchasing manager and the vendor.

ACTION STEPS

▲ Fight for informative board packets, avoiding the trap of too-thick reports.

▲ Be suspicious of segment reporting when there are unexplained losses at the entity level.

▲ Be bold in asking for third-party verification for management's explanation of any unexpectedly results.

▲ Pay attention to even small changes in gross margin.

▲ Look for surprising relationships between net income and cash flows from operations.

The Role of Management Estimates

Management estimates can play an enormous role in how the financial position of an organization appears to third parties. Managers may find themselves doctoring estimates for any number of reasons, including to demonstrate an upward trend in earnings and asset values, or to smooth earnings. When managers manipulate estimates in an effort to show upward trends, the efforts are unsustainable and eventually collapse. Earnings management, in which managers over- or undervalue various estimates from year to year to reach specific targets, leads to reversing previously recorded distortions because overall asset valuations remain notionally anchored to the value of the underlying assets. Significant account types that are susceptible to management discretion include accounts receivable, inventory, and revenue recognition.

Accounts Receivable

The valuation of accounts receivable depends on management's estimation of the allowance for bad debt. The allowance for doubtful accounts can be estimated using a variety of measures. These include the consideration of collectibility of account balances in the aggregate based on how many days the balance has been outstanding, specific customer collection review, historical write-offs, or a blend of all three methods.

In considering collectibility of accounts based on the number of days the balances have been outstanding, management would start by running a list of accounts receivable that segregates balances into separate categories, such as accounts with balances outstanding 0–30 days, 30–60 days, 60–90 days, and more than 90 days. A report that outlines balances outstanding by the number of days is often referred to as an aging report, with each grouping of days described as an aging bucket. In determining the collectibility of various aging buckets, the presumption is that the most recent balances are much more collectible than the older balances. Thus, management is likely to presume that balances that are current, or 0–30 days outstanding, are mostly collectible, and may only reserve up to 5 percent for expected write-offs. Balances outstanding over 90 days may be presumed to be largely uncollectible, and management may choose to reserve 50 percent or more of the balances outstanding over 90 days as uncollectible. Unfortunately, there is no industry standard for typical percentages of reserve for uncollectibility to apply to the various aging buckets of receivables. Since there is so much discretion for management in determining the percentages to reserve for the various aging buckets, opportunities exist for distorting the asset valuation of accounts receivable.

When managers determine the allowance for bad debt based on specific customer accounts, qualitative factors of creditworthiness are considered, such as payment history, purchase volume, and the economic health of the customer. Evaluating the creditworthiness of every customer may be too time-consuming, so evaluation of specific customers may be done only on large balances, especially for those accounts with balances outstanding over 60 or 90 days.

A review of historical write-offs is a good place to start in determining the adequacy of the reserve for doubtful accounts because such a multiyear view brings to the surface any intentional manipulations by management in the current year. However, the precision of this method can be diminished if there have been changes in the credit-writing policies such that credit is eased in an effort to pump up sales volume. In an environment of loosening credit, organizations should anticipate increasing levels of write-offs of customer accounts.

Other warning signs of poor quality receivables include occasions when the time to receive collection on sales lengthens, receivables grow faster than sales, accounts receivable turnover decreases, or management increases its practice of converting accounts receivable to notes receivable.

Audit committee members can evaluate the integrity of the accounts receivable reserve for doubtful accounts by inquiring of management the methods used and the basis for conclusions on creditworthiness, with a preference toward a methodology that is a blend of percentage estimate, specific identification, and historical trends in write-offs.

Inventory

Inventory valuation is a factor of quantity and unit price of goods. Fraudulent inventory numbers can be achieved by falsifying inventory physical count tallies, whereas unit prices can be affected by either incorrectly stating acquisition prices or by failing to record losses in inventory valuation for obsolete inventory. The reserve for inventory obsolescence attempts to quantify the amount of inventory that has been in inventory so long that the value for which it can be sold is lower than the amount paid for it. Of the three methods of misstating inventory, underestimating the inventory obsolescence reserve is the most difficult to identify.

Inventory can be devalued because market conditions are such that prices dropped though either decreased demand or increased supply, because the goods in inventory are perishable and subject to spoilage, or because changes in technology are so swift that the product has been surpassed by subsequent product offerings. Because the sources of losses in inventory valuation can be so varied and difficult to quantify, it can be tempting for managers to understate inventory obsolescence amounts in an effort to improve the valuation of inventory. Audit committee members can delve into the quality of the estimate for inventory obsolescence by asking for reports on historical write-offs, slow-and-no-moving inventory, and even price-testing results.

Reviewing the history of product obsolescence write-offs may give audit committee members a sense of typical annual write-offs to help evaluate the reasonableness of current year inventory write-offs. However, if managers have been consistently underestimating product obsolescence, a trend analysis will not detect understatement of the obsolescence reserve in the current year. In such a case, more sophisticated reports that calculate the number of years on hand by part ferrets out inventory that is slow moving.

Slow-and-no-moving inventory reports are excellent tools to identify inventory parts that are most likely obsolete or close to it. A slow-moving inventory report lists all parts that have more inventory on hand than demand requires. What qualifies as slow moving varies among organizations and can include parts with inventory in excess of six months' demand or up to two years' demand. No-moving inventory reports list parts for which no movement has occurred, the period under review varying by organization, with the upper end typically being two years.

For example, at a Midwestern manufacturer, the slow-and-no-moving inventory report listed parts valued at a cost of approximately $500,000. The time period under review was two years. So the slow-moving inventory report, noting inventory at a value of approximately $300,000, listed parts for which quantities on hand exceeded two years' demand, while the no-moving inventory report, at a value of approximately $200,000, listed inventory parts that had no movement in the past two years. Such a report would indicate that up to $500,000 of inventory could be obsolete.

Another request audit committee members can make in considering the adequacy of the inventory obsolescence reserve is to review the results of the inventory price testing. This testing is primarily used by auditors to verify the valuation of inventory by comparing the prices listed in the inventory report to the invoices associated with the purchase of the parts. But when significant inventory obsolescence is an issue, auditors likely encounter many parts for which the invoices are unavailable because of the organization's document-retention practices.

At one particular manufacturer, for example, the price-testing effort revealed that a large number of parts were so old that original receipts could not be located, making the price testing a function not of verifying unit prices of inventory but of attributing the reduction in inventory value to obsolescence. In this instance, the auditor was seeking a modest sample size of 35, and the first batch of parts selected for price testing resulted in only 17 parts that had invoices available. The remaining parts were so old that the manufacturer no longer retained the invoices. Not to be deterred, the auditor selected a new sample group of parts, only half of which had supporting invoices. This process of dropping the sample and reselecting was repeated four times, but still the auditor was unable to complete the price-testing sample with 35 parts. Although the lack of invoices made the price testing challenging, the broader conclusion was that up to half of the parts could be assumed to be obsolete since their presence on the inventory-parts list exceeded the organization's document-retention policy.

Inventory price testing can reveal important patterns. Audit committee members looking to evaluate the soundness of management's reserve for product obsolescence might find valuable information by asking the auditor how many parts had to be dropped from the selection for price testing because of lack of supporting invoices.

Other clues that inventory has a growing obsolescence problem include decreasing inventory turnover either in the aggregate or by individual part, and/or increasing number-of-days-sales-in-inventory.

Revenue Recognition

Revenue recognition can be heavily influenced by management judgment. The SEC has issued guidelines to assist management in determining when revenue should be recognized. The standard specifies that "revenue generally is realized or realizable and earned when all of the following criteria are met":

> ➤ Persuasive evidence of an arrangement exists.

> ➤ Delivery has occurred or services have been rendered.

> ➤ The seller's price to the buyer is fixed or determinable.

> ➤ Collectibility is reasonably assured.[15]

Although having a standard for revenue recognition may seem to reduce ambiguity, much discretion on the part of management still exists. For some organizations, uncertainty arises because of ambiguity of ownership for the goods subject to sale. Organizations that have consignment sales to end users or distributors, or who have bill-and-hold arrangements, have to be careful about when revenue is earned because possession and ownership are not directly linked. For example, suppliers to Dell have on-site storage facilities at their manufacturing facilities to reduce the time of inventory ownership. By agreement with suppliers, ownership does not transfer to Dell until the parts move across specified lines marked onto the floor of a manufacturing facility, at which point ownership of the raw materials transfers from the supplier to Dell.

Ambiguity of ownership can also be at play when organizations accept cash in advance of work in the form of customer deposits. Organizations that do not properly account for deposits as liabilities could be overstating net worth. Therefore, audit committees should be keen to any practices that allow for customer deposits. Specifically, audit committee members should inquire if the sales process involves customers' paying deposits on large orders such that management could erroneously account for cash receipts as income.

Accounting for multiyear contracts can also make it challenging to decide in which year to record income. This is common for construction companies that have multiyear, multiphase building projects. Organizations may track progress internally under the cost method, such that, for instance, a $100,000 project could be deemed to be 25 percent completed when costs incurred reach $25,000. Progress of $25,000 into $100,000 could be expressed as a 25 percent burn rate, with burn rate referring to the progress of a project. However, going through a quarter of the expenses does not mean that a project is a quarter of the way done. Relying just on the cost basis of the project could hide overruns. Most organizations pair the cost basis of a project with internal evaluations of progress of the project. Outside evaluations, performed by engineers or inspectors, can be performed to provide additional assurance, especially for significant, high-dollar projects.

Multiyear contracts can also arise out of licensing agreements. Many organizations, including software companies like Microsoft, have declared their revenue-recognition policy to be posting any receipts as unearned income and then recording income evenly over the number of years under contract. Such a revenue-recognition policy may seem to be a fair and reasonable method. However, complexities arise for product sales that come with the right to receive upgrades, especially when the fair value of such upgrades does not exist. In such arrangements, a portion of the revenue could be deemed to remain unearned until the product upgrade is delivered. Because of the uncertainty in the number and timing of such upgrades, no objective standard has emerged to assist managers in determining the appropriate timing of recognition of income for future periods. Microsoft, for example, has decided to "recognize [income] on a straight-line basis over the estimated life of the software."[16]

Audit committees that encounter revenue-recognition discussions find that determination of the appropriate resolution is dictated by the matching principle that attempts to spread the process of revenue recognition over the periods that goods and services are delivered.

With so much variability possible in the timing of receipts, change of possession, and continuous product delivery, audit committee members need to be alert to the ability of management to manipulate earnings recognition and respond with additional skepticism, especially when financial performance reported appears better than expected.

ACTION STEPS

▲ Dig deeper on management estimates of accounts receivable, inventory, and revenue.

▲ For accounts receivable, understand what methods managers are using to evaluate the creditworthiness of customers.

▲ Look beyond historical accounts receivable write-offs when credit policies have loosened.

▲ Request additional information to evaluate adequacy of reserve for inventory obsolescence, such as the slow-/no-moving report and auditor's results for parts dropped from price-testing samples.

▲ Consider the ambiguity surrounding revenue recognition, especially for organizations with multiyear contracts and goods moving before or after receipt for sales orders.

CHAPTER SIX

Leverage Internal Audit and Outside Resources

SOLID REPUTATIONS take years to earn, but they can be destroyed with just one bad decision. No type of organization is immune to this risk. For example, nonprofits that experience lapses in internal controls that lead to the disclosure of internal control deficiencies suffer with fewer donations for years, according to Christine Petrovits, Catherine Shakespeare, and Aimee Shih.[1]

The oversight of auditors, financial statements, controls, risks, and other duties adds up to be an incredibly daunting task. A properly utilized internal audit function can serve as the audit committee's eyes and ears. In this chapter, we look at the internal audit mandate, internal audit oversight, setting the internal auditing budget, internal audit administration, and some signs of an ineffective internal audit function.

The Internal Audit Mandate

Any organization that has grown beyond the mom-and-pop business-management model has a need for some degree of an internal audit function because of the potential divergence between individual and organizational goals. At worst, organizations can suffer when managers put their own interests ahead of other stakeholders. Short of that, organizations can also find reaching strategic targets difficult when managers act innocuously but in an unsynchronized fashion that diminishes operational effectiveness. An active internal audit function can mitigate both malevolent and nonmalevolent misapplications of organizational resources.

Publicly traded companies have limited guidance on the precise duties of the internal audit function. Section 404(a) of the Sarbanes-Oxley Act of 2002, which applies to all companies that report to the SEC, creates a mandate that management assess and draw conclusions about internal controls over financial reporting (ICFR). Adherence to this requirement creates the need for an internal audit function even if an internal audit department is not formally established.

The New York Stock Exchange goes a step farther than SOX. In its *Listed Company Manual*, the organization not only requires an internal audit function but also recommends separate meetings between audit committee members and internal auditors. Audit committees must "meet separately, periodically, with management, with internal auditors (or other personnel responsible for the internal audit function) and with independent auditors."[2]

The commentary to this clause reads: "To perform its oversight functions most effectively, the audit committee must have the benefit of separate sessions with management, the independent auditors and those responsible for the internal audit function. As noted herein, all listed companies must have an internal audit function. These separate sessions may be more productive than joint sessions in surfacing issues warranting committee attention."[3]

Regardless of an organization's status as a publicly traded or privately held organization, governance demands the existence of some degree of internal audit function, whether executed by a dedicated internal audit department or by a group of managers or hired consultants.

The Institute of Internal Auditors (IIA) defines internal audit activity as: "A department, division, team of consultants, or other practitioner(s) that provides independent, objective assurance and consulting services designed . . . to evaluate and improve the effectiveness of governance, risk management and control processes."[4]

The IIA definition reveals a few important issues. First, it indicates that the function can be organized internally or that it can make use of external resources. Second, the internal audit encompasses an array of duties, at a minimum including assurance-type services such as financial, performance, compliance, system security, and due diligence engagements. It also may go beyond assurance services to include consulting services intended to add value and improve an organization's governance, risk management, and control processes. Finally, the IIA definition specifies that the internal audit services be independent, which can be best assured when internal audit oversight is performed by the audit committee or the board rather than by management.[5]

Unfortunately, many companies focus their internal audit activities almost exclusively on external financial reporting, with the result being that improvements to governance, risk, and controls don't receive the necessary attention, exposing audit committee members and directors to possible claims of negligence.

ACTION STEPS

▲ Make sure your organization has an internal audit function, even if it is performed by outside consultants.

▲ Ensure independence by having the internal auditor report directly to the audit committee, rather than to *management*.

▲ Provide sufficient resources to the internal auditor to ensure that it can move beyond a compliance-centric focus and address operational, financial, and strategic initiatives.

Internal Audit Oversight

Internal audits assist the audit committee in carrying out its primary responsibility: ensuring that the organization is complying with its policies and procedures to best address risk areas. In an effort to maximize the benefits of having a dedicated internal audit function, audit committees can pull four primary levers: selecting and evaluating the chief audit executive (CAE), communicating with the CAE, setting the internal audit annual budget, and approving the internal audit program.

Selecting and Evaluating the Chief Audit Executive

The CAE sets the tone for the entire internal audit function and, therefore, is the single largest determining factor in the success of the internal audit mandate. Although all business leaders are expected to possess appropriate experience and skills, it is integrity, vision, and courage that serve as additional imperative qualities of a great CAE.

Integrity

The personal integrity of the CAE predicates the effectiveness of the internal audit function because audit testing, in both the design of tests and the interpretation of results, is far from a black-and-white matter. Discretion is required when auditors design tests that honor the spirit of audit standards and when auditors evaluate the seriousness of testing results that deviate from standards.

Integrity goes beyond a statement of values. It involves taking action based on one's convictions that can be unpopular and could adversely affect one's own personal wealth or prestige. Integrity is best demonstrated by prior actions. An audit leader who fails to exemplify the highest moral and ethical standards can cause all auditors on the team to underperform. So, audit committee members should review a candidate's prior work experience for instances in which the candidate's actions demonstrated a commitment to stated values.

Vision

The audit committee and the CAE need to share a clear vision of the direction in which they believe the organization should head. The internal audit mandate includes a broad spectrum of responsibilities, including evaluation and analysis of an organization's compliance, operational, regulatory, and strategic roles. Since most organizations operate with budget constraints, it is likely that tough choices must be made on how limited resources will be applied to the wide variety of goals. The audit committee should evaluate the CAE's priorities to ensure a good fit. Together, the CAE's and audit committee's shared vision can prove to be a powerful inspiration that motivates others within and outside the internal audit department.

Courage

A courageous CAE has the strength to operate in his or her role in support of both integrity and vision. Since not all news is good news, CAEs must be trusted to provide candid feedback that may be unpopular with some. Courageous CAEs push away concerns of personal gains such as future promotions and compensation in order to provide the value the internal audit function has to offer.

Alleviating CAE concerns about personal retribution for speaking the truth can be built into the governance structure, with special attention given to ensuring that the CAE's reporting lines run outside of management's reach.

As a case in point, we know of one nonprofit organization that had a director running inappropriate expenses through the company despite the presence of a capable CAE. The director in question not only served in management but also set the CAE's compensation.

Such conflicts of interest can set up a CAE for failure, and audit committees should take care to ensure that the CAE can speak frankly without fear of retribution, which means not only setting up a culture of truth but also reviewing candidates for past experiences that demonstrate courage.

Communicating with the Chief Audit Executive

Those conducting the internal audit function regularly prepare reports of audit findings along with a set of recommendations to improve control deficiencies. Without the endorsement of the audit committee, internal audit findings could be ignored by management who may find the internal audit report embarrassing and the recommendations for correction unappealing. To improve the benefit of having an internal audit function, it is important that the internal audit group has a direct reporting line to the audit committee so that internal audit reports find an audience beyond the managers evaluated by the internal audit group.

To receive the most candid responses, it is recommended that the audit committee meet directly with the CAE without management present. In speaking with the CAE, the audit committee should explicitly address:

> ➤ Potential changes to the scope of the internal audit function. This is an excellent time to review the internal audit charter that describes the internal audit's stated objectives, general activities of internal audit, and internal audit reporting lines between the CAE and management, board members, the compliance group (if one exists), and legal counsel.

> ➤ Issues that the internal auditor believes warrant the audit committee's attention, such as difficulties with management or fraud red flags.

> ➤ Draft reports to management prepared by the internal auditor.

> ➤ Management corrective action plans to address noted deficiencies.

> ➤ Results of prior management corrective action plans.

Setting the Internal Audit Annual Budget

Value and cost are often directly correlated, and the effectiveness of internal audit often increases with additional resources. With increasing demands on organizational resources, however, internal audit budgets are getting squeezed along with other cost centers. Yet the demands placed on the internal audit function are increasing in direct correlation to increased regulatory and judicial action. To maximize the cost benefits of internal audit resources, audit committees can assist the CAE in setting the annual auditing budget and prioritizing the key objectives and risks.

In order to promote auditor independence, audit committees should ensure that the internal audit budget is developed outside the influence of management. In addition, audit committees should also be sure that sufficient resources are set aside in the budget for using third-party resources in case sensitive assurance areas arise that are better handled by resources outside the organization.

ACTION STEPS

▲ Select a CAE who exemplifies the highest standards of integrity, courage, and vision, seeking out candidates who can't be bought.

▲ Assist the CAE in setting priorities so that budget constraints don't impair audit effectiveness.

▲ Protect the budgeting process from management influence to improve auditor independence.

Approving the Internal Audit Program

Internal audit is not intended to provide absolute assurance. The only way to do that would be to test 100 percent of transactions during the reporting period. For expediency and cost efficiency, internal controls are relied upon to reduce the likelihood that errors occur and to increase the likelihood that any errors that do occur are identified in the normal course of business.

The evaluation of internal controls is twofold. First, the adequacy of the internal control design must be evaluated. Controls, defined as policies, procedures, and supporting activities within a process, should be evaluated to ensure that standard procedures provide reasonable assurance regarding the achievement of objectives. Second, the effective and consistent operation of the controls throughout the period must be tested. The audit committee should be comfortable that a well-balanced testing approach exists in the audit program, including analytical review procedures, observation, inquiry, reperformance of management tasks, and reconciliation.

There are three broad categories of focus in an internal audit program: financial reporting, operations, and compliance. In the post-SOX era, many resources for publicly traded companies have been applied to address controls over financial reporting, at times to the detriment of operational and compliance testing. In reviewing the internal audit program, the audit committee should consider the appropriateness of allocation of resources between the three separate areas of financial reporting, operations, and compliance. Furthermore, the audit committee should ensure that risks identified in the risk assessment are pulled into the audit program to be sure that identified mitigating controls are operating effectively. (See Chapter 8 for more information on risk assessments.)

Financial Reporting

Cycles of weak external financial reporting remain fresh in the public's mind. Inadequate reporting by Enron and WorldCom in the early 2000s and by Lehman Brothers, Merrill Lynch, American International Group, Washington Mutual, Wachovia, and other financial institutions in the late 2000s led to significant investor shock. Publicly traded companies are not the only organizations subject to financial reporting requirements. Privately held businesses, while not subject to SOX, must often provide financial reports to lenders and regulators. Nonprofit organizations are expected to provide adequate financial reports to donors and grantors.

Ensuring adequate, accurate, and timely financial reporting is a primary duty of the audit committee. With regard to internal controls over financial reporting, audit committees should determine whether processes and procedures are in place and operating effectively to produce accurate and adequate financial reporting to third parties, including audited financial statements and public filings.

Operations

Organizations are challenged to take bold actions and execute creative approaches to stay ahead of the competition and meet their operational objectives. Operational controls support the achievement of operating objectives that are central to an organization's reason to exist, including performance goals and safeguarding resources against loss.

Many for-profit entities favor operational controls that are set up to support profitability, strategy, revenue growth, client satisfaction, and cash flows, which satisfy creditors, investors, and funding sources. Nonprofit organizations, on the other hand, are more likely to set up operational controls designed to ensure that benefits are realized in pursuit of the entity's purpose or mission.

Regardless of the type of organization, an internal audit program of operational controls should include the internal audit's evaluation of the extent to which management is able to adequately address the following questions:

> ➤ What risks are lurking that could prevent us from reaching our revenue targets?
> ➤ Do we foster healthy internal reporting relationships for sound decision-making purposes?
> ➤ What culture do we have, and do we like it?
> ➤ Is our strategy effectively deployed?
> ➤ Do we truly know our clients' needs?
> ➤ How do stakeholders view us?
> ➤ What opportunities exist to improve financial results?
> ➤ How can we become more cost efficient?
> ➤ What can we do to enhance our competitive position?
> ➤ Are we innovative leaders?

In the event of negative responses, leaders should assess where improvements can be made, including the possibility of creating new operational controls or directives that help the organization meet its goals and fulfill its mission.

Compliance

Compliance programs address both internal and external compliance matters. Compliance with laws and regulations are external matters. Compliance with organization-specific policies and procedures—such as assessing the effectiveness of the corporate compliance and ethics program, or the processing of the company's whistle-blowing program—relate to internal matters. Both types of compliance are important and should be addressed in the internal audit program based on a risk assessment.

With regard to external compliance matters, all organizations are subject to some level of compliance requirements. At a minimum, organizations must deal with tax and labor-law compliance. Organizations that operate on credit must satisfy lenders with reporting on various debt requirements, which may include specific debt covenants that must be met to ward off defaults as well as to ensure continued financing. Nonprofits may have enhanced compliance requirements based on government funding or other funding source reporting requirements.

The internal audit program regarding compliance should have steps in place to ensure that additional and evolving requirements are included in the organization's compliance program. Steps can include having specific personnel assigned to updates, scheduling a time to look for updates, and sending staff to training on updates. In addition, the audit committee should check the internal audit program to confirm the adequacy and effective execution of compliance controls.

ACTION STEPS

▲ Be sure the internal audit program includes steps that challenge the CFO and other managers tasked with implementation of internal controls regarding the design of controls.

▲ Ensure that the internal audit program flows from a risk assessment.

▲ Take time to understand essential elements of the internal audit program prior to approval, such as the types of procedures to be performed and the areas of financial reporting, operations, and compliance.

Internal Audit Administration

The internal audit charter established by an organization serves as the foundation for solid internal audit function. Audit committees should insist that internal auditors create a charter built upon principles similar to those outlined in the IIA's *International Standards for the Professional Practice of Internal Auditing.* The IIA standards include statements of basic requirements for the professional practice of internal auditing and for evaluating the effectiveness of its performance. The IIA standards address numerous topics related to internal auditing, including guidance on setting engagement objectives, scope, work programs, resource allocation, and supervision.[6] Although these standards provide no absolute assurance against errors and poor judgments, they can go a long way toward mitigating associated risks.

Organizing an Internal Audit Function

The internal audit function can be organized in a multitude of ways. There is no single suggested model, because the effectiveness and efficiency of the function depends on the size, industry, and culture of the organization. Regardless, those performing the internal audit function should report directly to the board or a committee of the board. After finalizing the reporting relationship between those performing the internal audit function and the board and its committees, management, with board approval, must then decide how to staff the internal audit function. There are three general approaches:

1. In-house: Employees of the organization are tasked with the function.

2. Outsourced: Third-party resources are used to fulfill the function.

3. Cosourced: A combination of employees and third-party resources fulfill the function.

In-House Function

Many larger organizations prefer to staff the internal audit function with employees. The leader of this group is usually the chief audit executive or the chief internal auditor. This individual serves as the primary internal auditor and reports to the audit committee. In some organizations the internal audit function might be carried out by just one person; in more-complex organizations it can be a team of hundreds.

A benefit of the in-house model is that the organization has more control tools at its disposal to motivate internal auditors that extend beyond compensation. Of course this can also work as a negative, as auditors are at a greater risk of losing their objectivity because of the enhanced interpersonal relationships unavoidable among coworkers. This lack of objectivity could impair the necessary skepticism required of the internal audit function. Another potential negative is that in-house auditors adapt to internal processes and systems such that, over time, they lose perspective that comes from exposure to multiple control environments. This risk can be mitigated with hearty training and rotation of the auditor's workload between reporting entities within larger, more complex, organizations.

Outsourced Function

This is a popular route for smaller organizations that cannot justify a full-time equivalent employee year-round for the internal audit function. Although no universal test exists for this threshold, organizations with less than $250 million in annual revenue typically fall in this category. Scale of the organization aside, the choice to staff internally or to outsource may be dictated by the complexity of the operations and other risk exposures. Even organizations large enough to have an in-house internal audit function may choose to outsource for access to certain specialized or sensitive matters. A potential downside to this model is higher costs, which is common with the use of third-party service providers.

If the decision has been made to use outside resources, care must be taken in selecting an objective service provider. This is easier said than done since third-party contractors can be aligned with an internal sponsor, thus introducing a potential lack of independence. Mitigating this risk requires the audit committee to independently procure the right resources without input from management. Even then, one could argue that the board or audit committee's hiring of an outside resource impairs independence because the third-party resource could be called upon to evaluate the performance of the board and audit committee in its set of procedures. There is no easy way around this, so the board and audit committee need to be mindful of the independence of any service provider during the hiring process.

Cosourced Function

This is an increasingly popular model because it can work upon the strengths of both the in-house and outsourced models. Utilizing outside resources offers a greater capacity to adapt to bursts in audit activities. For example, public companies subject to SOX requirements must assess their ICFR at the end of their fiscal years to evaluate the operating effectiveness of their ICFR. This triggers surges in audit activity, and tapping outside resources is a viable alternative to handle these seasonal variations in workload. Other advantages to cosourcing include acquiring specialized expertise as needed and injecting an outside perspective to provide alternative approaches and viewpoints.

A significant challenge with cosourcing can be a lack of coordination between the CAE and the third-party project leader. It is vital for the audit committee to clearly designate the leader of the internal audit function. The ideal reporting relationship is usually the outside resource reporting to the CAE; however, there could be circumstances under which the audit committee may want the third-party resource to report directly to it, such as evaluations of the internal audit function and sensitive matters where the CAE's independence and objectivity are in doubt.

No matter which reporting structure or staffing model is adopted, precautions must be taken to ensure the effectiveness of the internal audit function.

Signs of an Ineffective Internal Audit Function

Those who conduct the internal audit must be held accountable, just like all others in an organization are. In an effort to maximize the benefit of the internal audit function, the audit committee should be mindful of some common pitfalls that can render an internal audit function ineffective. These include:

> ➤ Insufficient resources
> ➤ A "check the boxes" mentality
> ➤ A lack of surprise audits
> ➤ Failure to address sensitive areas

Insufficient Resources

Inadequate resources can nullify the benefits of a well-staffed audit department and a well-designed audit program. Yet the strength of an internal audit department cannot be judged merely by the number of people on staff, but rather by asking: Does the staff have the right mix of credentials, experience, and skills to get the job done?

Allotting insufficient resources for the internal audit function can lead to harm for a company's reputation. For example, American Strategic Minerals Corp. reported in its annual report to the SEC, "Management has determined that our internal audit function is significantly deficient due to insufficient qualified resources to perform internal audit functions." The disclosure added, "Because of its inherent limitations, internal control over financial reporting may not prevent or detect misstatements."[7]

Such a declaration announces to trade partners, including shareholders and lenders, that external financial reporting could be unreliable. Markets don't like unreliable financial information and are likely to charge a premium for financing and discount share prices to account for the increased risk, as noted in the research paper "The Effect of SOX Internal Control Deficiencies on Firm Risk and Cost of Equity." However, organizations with effective internal control or firms that remediate previously reported internal control deficiencies are rewarded with a significantly lower cost of equity.[8]

Audit committee members must work together with the internal audit control team to ensure that resources are being used effectively. If adjustments are needed the audit committee should work with management to redress any areas of concern.

A "Check the Boxes" Mentality

Over time, it can be difficult for organizations to proceed rigorously through the internal audit function, with some organizations devolving into a "check the boxes" mentality. The causes can be many, including stale procedures outlined in the audit program, a lack of management follow-up on internal audit findings, and external auditors who blindly accept the work of the internal auditors.

Although all of these situations can limit the effectiveness of internal auditing, perhaps the most dangerous is when the external auditor accepts without conviction the work of the internal auditors. For example, the Public Company Accounting Oversight Board found a weakness with Big Four auditing firm Deloitte & Touche LLP, saying it used the work of an internal audit without adequately assessing the sufficiency of the internal audit procedures and that it failed to adequately respond to the findings of these procedures.[9]

Audit committee members should regularly review the performance of those conducting internal audit to ensure that they are acting objectively and with rigor. In addition, the audit committee should ensure that management is following up on any areas of concern revealed in the auditor's findings.

A Lack of Surprise Audits

Although the mainstay of auditing techniques rests upon testing large samples of data at scheduled intervals, great value can be extracted when interim tests are performed on a surprise basis. The element of surprise introduces a desirable trait to the audit program because the auditee does not know the approach, including testing thresholds, used by the auditor. This does not mean that the auditor cannot inform a department in advance about upcoming fieldwork, but rather that the auditor does not disclose how it intends to conduct the audit or the scope of the work to be performed.

For example, a surprise audit approach can be aided greatly in terms of effectiveness and efficiency with controls available through the information technology department, especially those information technology tools that relate to access, version, change management, log reviews, and continuous monitoring. Audit committee members should understand that testing these areas on a surprise basis can be particularly effective because there can tend to be unevenness in compliance with these controls, with a great deal of the compliance effort expended just prior to the normal audit cycle. By testing compliance duties apart from routine compliance evaluations, unscheduled audits can provide more information on the level of compliance and a higher degree of confidence. The benefits of the surprise audit approach can be further reinforced when surprise audit procedures are changed from period to period.

Failure to Address Sensitive Areas

Some people look for ways to avoid the most sensitive, controversial aspects of life. In the business world, this cuts at the heart of ethics, leadership lines, competency, and accountability. As a result, many organizations do not heartily assess these areas head-on for fear of jeopardizing friendships, internal repercussions, retaliation, or other career setbacks. Yet these are the very areas that the board and the audit committee members need to understand and assess, with the help of the internal audit function as the independent evaluator.

Although the internal audit cannot in practice examine 100 percent of the organization's data points, extra care should be given to examine even those areas that may cause embarrassment. Audit committee members should work together to ensure that internal auditors are investigating those areas of the organization that may prove sensitive for management, regardless of whether management may wish for those areas to be explored.

ACTION STEPS

▲ Provide adequate resources to the internal audit.

▲ Be on the lookout for the complacency that would foster an audit function that is merely going through the motions.

▲ Encourage the liberal use of surprise audits to supplement scheduled testing.

▲ Outlaw sacred cows, ensuring that no person, function, department, or strategy is exempt from internal audit activities, including the audit committee and the board of directors.

Chapter Seven

Satisfy Regulators and Other Stakeholders

An organization's success hinges on the continued support of its stakeholders, with perhaps few things more alarming for board members than losing the faith of stakeholders. Board directors at Apple and Wal-Mart, for example, found this to be true with front-page scandals arising from supply-chain mishaps.[1] Apple has been widely criticized for its environmental record, with environmental groups charging that the company has consistently looked the other way when it comes to pollution and toxic discharge up and down its supply chain, particularly in China. Similarly, Wal-Mart was blasted for its record in China after mislabeling conventionally raised pork as organic. Both companies know all too well the sting that comes from alienating the public's expectations.

Effective boards seek to integrate stakeholders' interest into the company's strategies, policies, and actions, so that win–win business scenarios that manage to generate revenue, create operating efficiencies, attract capital, and reach objectives emerge. If accomplished, companies are rewarded with:

> ➤ A stronger public image.
> ➤ Greater customer loyalty.
> ➤ Reduced employee turnover.

- ➤ Healthy vendor relationships.
- ➤ Favorable capital options.
- ➤ Fewer adverse regulatory actions.

This chapter looks at the full range of stakeholders—regulators, investors, creditors, insurers, communities, vendors, employees, and customers—to better understand their goals and likely areas of concern.

Regulators

Although directors need to be cognizant of their stakeholder relations, regulators often dominate audit committee stakeholder concerns because of the various laws, regulations, and other compliance criteria that must be satisfied. Publicly traded companies have given a great deal of attention to SOX-related governance issues. Yet with less than 1 percent of companies publicly listed,[2] the majority of boards must be attentive to laws and regulations that reach beyond Sarbanes-Oxley.

Every organization is subject to some degree of regulation, from taxation compliance to employment law to industry-specific regulation by such entities as the Food and Drug Administration or the Environmental Protection Agency. The more jurisdictions and industries in which a company operates, the more laws and regulations to which it must adhere.

Efforts to be in compliance with laws and regulations can vary greatly by industry. Yet there are laws and regulations, such as common law and the Federal Sentencing Guidelines, that apply to all organizations. This section also addresses specific regulatory concerns for publicly traded companies and global enterprises.

Common Law

Two of a director's most elemental fiduciary responsibilities stem from the common law duties of loyalty and care (see Chapter 2). As we have discussed, duty of loyalty suggests that directors not put their own interests before the corporation's. Duty of care demands that directors exercise good judgment, acting in good faith and in the best interests of the corporation. Directors can defend the duty of care by demonstrating that they exercised the care an ordinary person would use in the same situation. Courts have looked at the existence of an adequate compliance program in determining if directors have satisfied the common law duty of care.

In the landmark case *In re Caremark International Inc. Derivative Litigation*, the Delaware Court of Chancery decided that the members of Caremark's board of directors breached the fiduciary duty of care for their failure to exercise oversight, in that the board failed to attempt to ensure that a reasonable information and reporting system existed, including compliance programs. The 1996 decision determined that directors may be held liable for a breach of duty of care if they knew or even should have known that employees were breaking the law or if they failed to make a good-faith effort to prevent employees from breaking the law. The settlement of the case called for more board director and committee member oversight to ensure that employees abide by the law.

ACTION STEPS

▲ Satisfy duty of care by exercising good judgment and ensuring the adequacy of the organization's compliance program.

▲ Discharge the duty of loyalty by putting the interests of the organization above personal goals.

▲ Provide proper oversight of employees with the understanding that directors may be held liable for employees who fail to abide by the law.

Federal Sentencing Guidelines

Shrewd boards are attentive to the provisions of Federal Sentencing Guidelines because qualifying organizations are eligible for a 95 percent reduction in sentencing if an organization runs afoul of the law and commits one of a wide spectrum of white-collar crimes, including:

> Embezzlement
> Mail fraud, wire fraud, Internet fraud
> Bank fraud, money laundering
> Mortgage fraud, real estate fraud
> Securities violations
> Government contract fraud
> Tax fraud

Federal Sentencing Guidelines apply to public and private companies, as well as nonprofits and all other types of organizations, making them a topic of interest to all boards. When courts consider granting sentencing reductions under the guidelines, they take into account whether an effective compliance program is in place. The guidelines define an effective compliance program as one that is reasonably designed, implemented, and enforced so that it generally is effective in preventing and detecting criminal conduct. Crucial elements that support an effective compliance program are often referred to as the seven minimum requirements of an effective compliance and ethics program:

1. **Establishing Standards:** An organization's standards and procedures must be designed to be reasonably capable of preventing and detecting criminal conduct. A code of conduct and ethics policy satisfy this requirement.

2. **Assigning Responsibility:** The Federal Sentencing Guidelines expect that an organization's governing authority exercises reasonable oversight with respect to the implementation and effectiveness of the program. "Governing authority" typically refers to the board of directors, with many organizations placing their compliance programs

under the control of audit committees. Although many boards and audit committees delegate the day-to-day operations of the compliance program, audit committees should receive updates from those responsible for day-to-day responsibilities.

3. Exercising Due Diligence in Hiring: Hiring the right person serves a critical role in implementing an effective compliance program. The Federal Sentencing Guidelines require that the organization "use reasonable efforts not to include within the substantial authority personnel of the organization any individual whom the organization knew, or should have known through the exercise of due diligence, has engaged in illegal activities or other conduct inconsistent with an effective compliance and ethics program." Reasonable screening efforts can include background checks, education verification, and other steps prescribed by bond underwriters.

4. Communicating the Policy: The guidelines intend for organizations to communicate the compliance policy to anyone who could adversely affect the organization through misconduct. Boards should ensure that the compliance policy is communicated to all levels of the organization, from entry-level position up through the board of directors. Organizations should not forget about communicating the compliance policy to vendors and independent contractors who can also negatively impact the organization.

5. Achieving Compliance: The guidelines do not allow an organization to satisfy requirements merely by creating a set of policies without regard to effectiveness. Organizations can satisfy the achieving compliance standard by having an internal audit department (or outside consultants who perform the internal audit function), with the audit committee periodically briefed on adequacy of program effectiveness.

6. Taking Disciplinary Action: The courts look closely at how organizations respond to deviations in the compliance program, with particular attention paid to the organization's investigation protocol. A properly implemented investigation protocol, which may result in disciplinary action, must include the leadership of legal counsel to ensure that investigations are performed routinely and consistently.

7. Responding Appropriately: The guidelines expect organizations to learn from their mistakes by identifying the weaknesses in the control system and making modifications to prevent similar failures in the future. Including a step in the investigation protocol to consider necessary changes to business processes or controls addresses this requirement.

Periodic Assessment

In addition to adequate design of a compliance program, Federal Sentencing Guidelines require that organizations periodically assess their compliance programs. The guidelines expect that organizations evaluate the risk that criminal conduct will occur and modify their actions and their compliance and ethics program accordingly. Including the risk of criminal misconduct in the risk-assessment step of risk management addresses this requirement.

Sentencing Guidelines for Smaller Organizations

Sentencing guidelines are scalable, with courts taking into account an organization's size when evaluating the adequacy of the steps taken to satisfy the seven minimum requirements of an effective compliance program. Accommodations for smaller organizations, as determined by the courts, can include reducing requirements for specific compliance staff, allowing informal training, and monitoring being integrated with routine reporting processes. Hence, while audit committee members of smaller organizations should remain cognizant of the requirements, they should be aware that the sentence-reducing benefits of the Federal Sentencing Guidelines could be available to organizations that do not have the elaborate compliance departments that larger organizations can afford to support.

ACTION STEPS

▲ Establish standards by drafting a sound code of conduct and ethics policy.

▲ Assign responsibility for the administration of the compliance program, with periodic board updates.

▲ Require adequate due diligence in hiring through background and reference checks.

▲ Communicate the policy by providing new-hire training and annual updates on the organization's code of conduct and ethics policy.

▲ Achieve compliance by routinely evaluating the results of periodic tests of internal controls.

▲ Exercise appropriate disciplinary action for violations, being mindful of consistency.

▲ Make appropriate responses to breaches in controls by modifying business practices to reduce the chances of recurrence.

Publicly Traded Companies

In the United States, although there are many governmental agencies at the local, state, and federal levels to help protect investors, one clearly is at the forefront: the U.S. Securities and Exchange Commission.

The mission of the SEC is to protect investors; maintain fair, orderly, and efficient markets; and facilitate capital formation. The SEC has stepped up enforcement efforts in response to a series of financial calamities, including:

> ➤ The subprime mortgage crisis of 2008, which exposed weaknesses in financial industry regulation and the global financial system, including an approximately $60 trillion credit default swap market that was not regulated by any agency of government.

> ➤ An abrupt end to a broad credit boom and the meltdown of many financial institutions in September 2008 as part of a rapid deterioration of the world economy.

> The SEC's failure to detect the $18 billion Ponzi scheme operated by Bernard Madoff, which came to light in December 2008.

> The "flash crash" of May 6, 2010, when the Dow Jones Industrial Average dropped about 600 points, only to recover those losses within minutes, which was suspected to be caused by "automated execution programs and algorithmic trading strategies," prompting the SEC to adopt new "trading curbs known as circuit breakers."[3]

As a result of these and other financial catastrophes, the SEC has undergone major changes, including the establishment of a newly structured Enforcement Division. Under the leadership of former Chairman Mary L. Schapiro, who served from January 2009 until December 2012, the SEC desired to restore confidence. Enforcement efforts are increasing dramatically. As Chairman Schapiro stated in a speech on February 5, 2010, in Washington, D.C., titled "Looking Ahead and Moving Forward":

While statistics are not the best way to measure success, the numbers are nonetheless telling. In our first 12 months, compared to the previous year, our output increased significantly. In that time:

- We sought more than twice as many temporary restraining orders and asset freezes (restraining orders: 79 compared to 36—a 119 percent increase) (asset freezes: 89 compared to 42—a 112 percent increase).

- We issued well over two times as many formal orders of investigation (558 compared to 245—a 128 percent increase).

- We obtained about $540 million more in disgorgement orders and more than twice as much in penalty orders (disgorgement orders: about $1.73 billion compared to about $1.19 billion—a 45 percent increase) (penalty orders: about $410 million compared to about $193 million—a 112 percent increase).

- And, we filed nearly 10 percent more actions overall, including nearly twice as many involving Ponzi-like schemes. (Overall actions: 725 compared to 665—a 9 percent increase) (Ponzi-specific: about 60 compared to about 35—a 71 percent increase).[4]

As enforcement efforts continue in earnest, audit committee members should be aware that what might once have been acceptable may no longer be tolerated by regulators. In particular, they should be aware of both the Securities Act of 1934 and the Sarbanes-Oxley Act of 2002, which are the two primary regulations that govern publicly traded companies.

The Securities Act of 1934

The Securities Act of 1934 has stood the test of time as one of the fundamental laws that continues to influence current-day best practices. The law requires companies with more than $10 million in assets that are owned by more than 500 shareholders to file annual reports (Form 10-K) and quarterly reports (Form 10-Q), and current reports on Form 8-K for a variety of specified events. Specified events reported on a Form 8-K include significant governance events such as failure to make required distributions, departure of directors or certain officers, election of directors, appointment of certain officers, amendments to the articles of incorporation or bylaws, and waivers to any company code of ethics.

The Sarbanes-Oxley Act of 2002

As we have discussed, the Sarbanes-Oxley Act of 2002 has become part of the common vocabulary of corporate governance. In place for more than a decade, SOX has become the driving force behind compliance efforts. Sarbanes-Oxley contains several sections that relate to closer scrutiny of stock analysts and credit agencies, while others specify more stringent sentencing for white-collar crime. Most significantly from a corporate governance perspective for officers and directors, SOX provisions fall into two broad categories: auditor independence and corporate responsibility.

> **Auditor Independence:** SOX seeks to promote auditor independence by prohibiting auditing firms from providing nonaudit services, such as consulting, to the same client. These sections specify mandatory auditor rotation for the lead and concurring audit part-

ners every five years, as well as a direct reporting line between external auditors and the audit committee.

> **Corporate Responsibility:** Audit committee members must understand the responsibilities of the C-suite. The corporate responsibility provisions of SOX specify that a company's principal officers, typically the CEO and CFO, must certify and approve the accuracy and completeness of the company's financial reports on a quarterly basis. In addition, SOX requires that the company's principal officers provide assurance on the adequacy of the design and implementation of the ICFR.

The corporate responsibility provisions of SOX set a new standard of accountability for the content of financial records provided to the public. Senior officers can no longer distance themselves from the financial statements. The C-suite is now invested with ensuring the validity of internal controls over financial reporting, as well as the financial statements those internal processes produced.

When looking for a credible, respected, internal control framework, most publicly traded companies adopted the integrated framework of internal controls promulgated by the Committee of Sponsoring Organizations (COSO), a private-sector organization dedicated to supporting those in governance on matters related to risk management, internal controls, and fraud deterrence. While there are other internal control frameworks, the COSO internal controls framework is by far the most widely adopted.

COSO Internal Control—Integrated Framework COSO defines internal controls as: "A process, effected by an entity's board of directors, management, and other personnel, designed to provide reasonable assurance regarding the achievement of objectives in the following categories:

1. Effectiveness and efficiency of operations
2. Reliability of financial reporting
3. Compliance with applicable laws and regulations"[5]

COSO states that internal controls consist of five interrelated components: control environment, risk assessment, control activities, information and communication, and monitoring. Audit committee members should be aware of the requirements and vocabulary surrounding these issues.

> **Control Environment:** An organization's control environment can be considered the tone at the top and refers to the management philosophy in setting standards for conduct. The control environment is influenced by the board as well, in the form of ethical leadership provided and in its commitment to selecting senior management on the basis of integrity and competence. A sound control environment provides a solid foundation for the remaining control components.

> **Risk Assessment:** The risk-assessment component addresses an organization's need to anticipate adverse outcomes that negatively affect stakeholders. The risk-assessment process allows organizations to consider all risks, internal and external, and address significant risks in the organization's strategic and operational goals.

> **Control Activities:** An organization's control activities refer to the policies and procedures in place to enforce management's directives. Control activities include preventive and detective controls, such as a whistle-blower hotline, surprise audits, reconciliations, and segregation of duties.

> **Information and Communication:** Information and communication refers to the specific way an organization assimilates important financial, operational, and compliance information and passes along pertinent information to those who need it. The information and communication component is central to the important governance concept of information flow and decision rights. Board directors can address this component by ensuring that all decision makers have adequate data to carry out their responsibilities and that reporting lines are clear. Satisfying this component may mean updating internal reports at all levels, including the board packet.

> **Monitoring:** The monitoring component is included in the COSO integrated framework because it acknowledges the need for an internal control system to be evaluated and updated periodically for optimal results. Monitoring activities include independent evaluations of internal controls as well as regular management oversight performed in the course of its duties.[6]

ACTION STEPS

▲ Evaluate external auditor effectiveness by assessing the degree of candid feedback and suggestions for improvements that can be acted upon.

▲ Consider auditor rotations at intervals shorter than those mandated by law.

▲ Make determinations on auditor independence in the context of formal and informal work and personal relationships.

▲ Promote an ethical work environment by selecting senior management on the basis of integrity and competence.

▲ Provide oversight for risk-management activities and challenging risk appetites.

Relation of COSO and Federal Sentencing Guidelines

While most publicly traded companies have embraced the COSO integrated internal control framework, many privately held organizations believe that the COSO standards don't apply to them because so much emphasis has been placed on how well the COSO framework supports SOX compliance. Federal Sentencing Guidelines show how all organizations, public and private, benefit from an effective compliance program because of the advantages in sentencing for many white-collar crimes. Figure 7.1 illustrates how the seven minimum requirements of the guidelines are aligned with the COSO system, reinforcing the need for all organizations to maintain effective compliance programs.

COMPONENTS	COSO	GUIDELINES
Control Environment		
Management	❑ Sets the ethical tone ❑ Leads by actions, such as rewarding ethical comduct while punishing unethical actions	❑ Sanctions for knowing, tolerating, or condining improper conduct ❑ Rewards for cooperation and contrition ❑ Due diligence requirement ❑ Upper management oversight of compliance program
Integrity and Ethical Values	❑ Code of Ethics ❑ Mechanism to encourage employee reporting	❑ Code of Ethics ❑ Additional reporting mechanisms
Human Resources	❑ Hiring those who demonstrate integrity ❑ Consistent discipline	❑ Nondelegation of authority to those with criminal tendencies ❑ Consistent discipline
Risk Assessment	❑ Objectives related to operations, financial reporting, and compliance ❑ Identification and analysis of relevant risks ❑ A strategy to manage risks	❑ Incentives to maintain internal controls ❑ Identification of industry-specific risks
Control Activities	❑ Policies and procedures to help ensure that management's directives are followed	❑ Standards and procedures capable of reducing the prospect of criminal conduct ❑ Determination of modifications needed to prevent future problems
Information and Communication	❑ The identification, capture, and communication of pertinent information in an appropriate format and time frame	❑ Effective communication of standards and procedures to all employees and other agents ❑ Required training or distribution of publications ❑ Establishment of additional reporting mechanisms (such as hotlines and helplines)
Monitoring	❑ Ongoing assessment of the internal control system	❑ Utilization of monitoring and auditing systems designed to detect criminal conduct.

Paul E. Fiorelli and Cynthia J. Rooney, "COSO and the Federal Sentencing Guidelines," *INTERNAL AUDITOR*, April 1997

Figure 7.1   Comparison of COSO and Federal Sentencing Guidelines components.

Global Enterprises

It is important for board directors and audit committee members for global enterprises to pay special attention to anticorruption efforts because government prosecution of bribery violations is increasing and can be very expensive.

Yet many businesses claim that they find it difficult to compete on a level playing field without engaging in corruption: "Nearly two in five polled business executives have been asked to pay a bribe when dealing with public institutions. Half estimated that corruption raised project costs by at least 10 percent. One in five claimed to have lost business because of bribes by a competitor."[7]

Although bribes can occur with both domestic and foreign business, global corruption has commanded significant attention from board directors and compliance officers alike, as the Department of Justice has ramped up efforts to enforce the Foreign Corrupt Practices Act (FCPA). The FCPA sets harsh penalties for extending bribes to foreign officials. Whereas bribes and grease payments to foreign officials used to be considered standard operating procedure for many global enterprises, much of that came to an end during the tenure of Mark Mendelsohn, who served as deputy chief of the fraud section at the Justice Department from 2004 to 2010. Mendelsohn zealously prosecuted corporate corruption under the FCPA, prompting many organizations to ramp up compliance budgets in order to be spared the multimillion-dollar fines Mendelsohn managed to get.

Awareness of regulatory scrutiny is a strong motivator for some board directors and audit committee members to improve oversight efforts. In addition, enforcement of the FCPA represents one of the more costly penalties governmental entities can impose on organizations involved in fraud. With record-breaking fines paid by Siemens at $800 million in 2008, $579 million by KBR/Halliburton in 2009, and $400 million by BAE in 2010, corporate oversight of corruption-prevention programs have captured the attention of most companies doing business globally.

The FCPA has two primary tenets: Don't bribe foreign officials, and keep accurate records with adequate controls. Penalties attach for violating each component, though fines in dollars and prison sentences are significantly higher for errors and omissions in record keeping and controls.

Transparency International has assembled data on leading industries and locations for public-sector corruption. The organization produced a 2011 index that measures perceived levels of public-sector corruption in 183 countries and territories. Countries with the lowest (worst) scores include Sudan, Myanmar, Somalia, Uzbekistan, Haiti, Venezuela, and Burundi (see Figure 7.2).

Transparency International tracks private-sector corruption in the Bribe Payers Index (see http://bpi.transparency.org/research/bpi/overview). The Bribe Payers Index measures the perceived likelihood that companies from 28 of the world's largest economies would offer bribes when doing business abroad. According to the index, the leading industries likely to offer private-sector bribes are public-works, construction, and utilities.

This is important information for audit committee members of global organizations, as detecting corruption is a crucial responsibil-

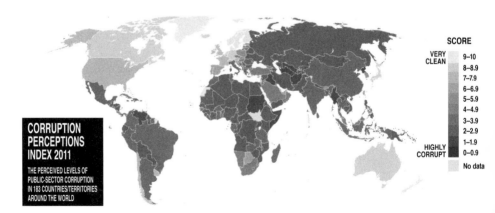

Figure 7.2   2011 Corruption Perceptions Index from Transparency International.
Source: Reprinted from Corruption Perceptions Index 2011. Copyright 2011 Transparency International: The Global Coalition Against Corruption. Used with permission. For more information, visit http://www.transparency.org.

ity. In terms of detecting corruption, two expense descriptions tend to be associated with bribes: gifts and travel. Under the compliance function, directors should be sure that compliance officers include the examination of the exchanges of gifts as part of their routine procedures. In general, certain gifts, such as items or services valued at less than $100, generally can be exchanged after approval has been granted by a government official. Gifts valued at more than $100 generally receive more scrutiny, and gifts given after approval is granted generally receive less scrutiny. Regardless of timing or amount, the legality of the exchange of a gift for a business favor often comes down to whether the public official had the right to say no. In other words, if the government official would have granted approval with or without the gift—say, for example, because all the conditions for permitting had been met—the gift would be more easily viewed as acceptable.

As for travel, the FCPA does not prohibit U.S. companies from paying for travel expenses of foreign officials that are legitimate business expenses, such as traveling to meet company personnel, to inspect products or company facilities, or to execute a contract. As outlined on the SEC Whistleblower Blog on December 6, 2010, travel-expense policies should be clearly established to simplify FCPA compliance.[8] A few of the suggestions listed that improve the likelihood of regulator approval include using a central travel office rather than allowing foreign officials or other third parties to book travel; having a clearly articulated travel policy; requiring detailed expense reports, especially when foreign officials are entertained; applying additional care when families or spouses of foreign officials are included in the travel plans; and employing consistent vigilance for international travel.

While the requirements for FCPA compliance are stringent by design, expectations should not be set that all corruption can be eradicated regardless of how exacting the compliance program. Mendelsohn stated in a March 17, 2011, *Wall Street Journal* interview, "If you have an effective, robust compliance program, you ought to be finding violations if you are doing business globally."[9] The critical effort board directors and audit committee members must make is to have that effective, robust compliance program that is considered so desirable by the courts, knowing that the compliance program most likely brings to the surface actionable violations.

By having a compliance program that is well designed and operating effectively, board directors have a better chance of discovering violations before law enforcement does. Voluntary disclosure programs exist that can provide reduced fines and sentences. The SEC and Justice Department both offer voluntary disclosure programs. In order to take advantage of such programs, organizations must be timely, they must be committed to restitution, and they must establish policies to prevent recurrence.

In some cases, organizations can qualify for deferred prosecution agreements (DPAs). DPAs are popular with the Justice Department and other government agencies. DPAs involve prosecutors dropping charges in exchange for full cooperation. Companies that do not have stringent compliance programs in place before a FCPA violation typically have the establishment of a compliance program as a condition of their DPA. The philosophy behind DPAs is that corrective action in the form of enhanced fraud-prevention programs is better than punishment.

While fines typically still attach to DPAs, accepting a DPA could keep an organization alive. For example, the accounting firm Arthur Andersen reputedly rejected the terms of a DPA offered and suffered the consequences: The firm no longer exists. The Justice Department's Filip Memo, which sets out Principles of Federal Prosecution of Business Organizations, provides guidance on how "full cooperation" is decided, specifically how "full cooperation" hinges on timeliness of disclosure.[10]

The FCPA deals only with bribes to foreign officials. New rules have come into play internationally through the United Kingdom Bribery Act that expand the definition of corruption to include bribes made to private officials. The UK Bribery Act, which went into force July 2011, indicates a change in public sentiment against corruption as a cost of doing business.

ACTION STEPS

▲ Avoid fines for poor record keeping by establishing a consistent document-retention policy.

▲ Promote ethical business practices by designing adequate controls aimed at preventing global corruption.

▲ Be mindful of gifts that border on bribes by creating a gift policy.

▲ Ensure travel for foreign officials does not constitute a bribe by:

  ◑ Using a central travel office rather than allowing foreign officials or other third parties to book travel.

  ◑ Having a clearly articulated travel policy, requiring detailed expense reports, especially when foreign officials are entertained.

  ◑ Exercising additional care when families or spouses of foreign officials are included in travel plans.

  ◑ Being just as vigilant in travel arrangements for foreign officials between foreign countries as you would be for travel between a foreign country and the United States.

Other Stakeholders

Stakeholders go beyond regulators, of course. Investors, creditors, insurers, communities, vendors, and customers also require the attention of the organization at every level. Audit committee members and board directors must strive to balance the needs of all stakeholders, who may have competing requirements.

Investors

Investors, as a stakeholder group, typically concern themselves with an enterprise's ability to build shareholder value. Maximizing return on investment drives many investors' view of a company's performance. Nonprofits have investors of sorts—donors who judge the effectiveness of an organization not by its profitability but rather by its ability to fulfill program objectives. Investor issues include executive compensation, fraud, return on investment, dividend policy, and transparency, since these factors often have a direct bearing on profitability.

Creditors

The stakeholder group of creditors is primarily concerned with an organization's ability to meet debt-service requirements. Many lenders specify loan covenants that track an organization's financial condition in the hope that an organization's likelihood to default can be predicted and addressed in advance. Board members find that creditors are most interested in an organization's efforts to preserve capital and meet debt-service requirements.

Insurers

Insurers are another part of the stakeholder group that audit committees must consider. Insurers have a vested interest in insured hazards, typically general liability, product liability, professional liability, and commercial property insurance. Bond underwriting procedures often address key factors identified by insurers that mitigate the risk exposure. Insurers are keenly interested in risk-management efforts (see Chapter 8).

Communities

Communities as stakeholders are concerned with an organization's ethical treatment of employees as well as of the environment. Community sentiment is also mindful of an organization's ability to contribute to the tax-revenue base, as well as its adherence to applicable laws and regulations. Audit committee members find that communities support the success of organizations that make the effort to promote fair employment practices, sustainability initiatives, and effective plans for profitability.

Vendors

Vendors as a stakeholder group are invested in the success of the organization and are primarily concerned with the sustained demand for their products. Vendors serve as critical partners in the success of an organization both through support in the cash-to-cash cycle through payment terms on purchase and through the reputation of the organization by supplying high-quality materials. To support the needs of vendors, audit committee members find that vendors, as much as any other stakeholder group, support governance efforts that prevent violations of regulatory edicts, bad business decisions, and fraud.

Customers

Customers have an interest in the ethical operation of a business enterprise and focus their attention on matters related to pricing, product safety, product development, and product availability. Because of the dispersed buying power of consumers, the government has stepped in occasionally in matters related to pricing, antitrust, and product safety. Audit committees and board directors should strive to balance the needs of shareholders and customers as they shape strategic and operational goals for the organization.

ACTION STEPS

▲ Look beyond the needs of regulators to address the concerns of other stakeholders.

▲ Be open to investor, vendor, and regulator concerns about executive compensation, fraud, return on investment, dividend policy, and transparency.

▲ Assuage creditor worries by monitoring debt covenants. Proactively communicate with creditors when problems are anticipated.

▲ Alleviate regulator, customer, and community anxieties by setting in place sound practices in pricing, employment, and product production.

CHAPTER EIGHT

Address Risk Proactively

MUCH OF THE FINANCIAL CRISIS of 2008 has been blamed on uncontained risk. Risk management has since emerged as a top priority for many stakeholder groups looking to hold those in governance accountable to proactively address risk. The audit committee, with its heightened awareness of fraud risk, plays a central role in risk management, even for those organizations that have impaneled a specific risk committee. In fact, the NYSE stated in 2004 that "while it is the job of the CEO and senior management to assess and manage the company's exposure to risk, the audit committee must discuss guidelines and policies to govern the process by which this is handled."[1]

This chapter tackles the essential topic of which questions audit committee members should ask about risk management and which actions they should take as they identify, respond to, and monitor risks that arise out of the financial reporting system.

It is important for audit committee members to understand that a consistent risk-management program can help all organizations, public or private. While the Public Company Accounting Oversight Board and the New York Stock Exchange enforce the consistent administration of a risk-management program, all organizations benefit from a systematic risk-management program because of sentencing leniency offered through the Federal Sentencing Guidelines and improved corporate debt ratings from Standard and Poor's. With that, this chapter also addresses risk-management frameworks, risk identification, risk-ranking tools, risk response, reporting risk, and risk-assessment follow-up.

Risk-Management Frameworks

Risk management is the process by which threats to an organization are identified, evaluated, prioritized, and reduced where possible. A methodical approach to risk management is suggested, and there are a variety of risk-management frameworks from which to choose. By far the most widely accepted risk-management framework comes from the Committee of Sponsoring Organizations (COSO) with its "Enterprise Risk Management—Integrated Framework," issued in 2004. This chapter explores the COSO framework, which is suitable for all organizations.

The Association of Certified Fraud Examiners also has a fraud risk-management framework, which addresses a more limited scope of risks by focusing specifically on fraud risks. Variations on standard risk-management frameworks are put into action by countless practitioners, each finding its own methodology and language to express the basic principles that serve as the foundation of risk management, including risk identification, risk ranking, risk remediation, and risk tracking.

Standard & Poor's also evaluates risk. When Standard & Poor's evaluates a risk-management program to determine corporate debt ratings, it asks organizations questions in these seven areas:

1. What are the company's top risks, how big are they, and how often are they likely to occur? How often is the list of top risks updated?

2. What is management doing about top risks?

3. What size quarterly operating or cash loss has management and the board agreed is tolerable?

4. Describe the staff responsible for risk-management programs and their place in the organizational chart. How do you measure the success of risk-management activities?

5. How would a loss from a key risk affect incentive compensation of top management and planning or budgeting?

6. What discussions about risk management have taken place at the board level or among top management when strategic decisions were made in the past?

7. Give an example of how your company responded to a recent "surprise" in your industry. How did the surprise end up affecting your company differently than what is known about the effect on other similar organizations?[2]

Board and audit committee members should ask these same questions of their own risk-management programs to be sure the chosen risk-management framework for the organization conforms to best practices in the field.

Risk Identification

In a broad sense, risks can be categorized as either macroeconomic (those risks that threaten organizational goals that stem from sources outside the direct control of the organization) or microeconomic (those risks that are specific to the organization). Examples of macroeconomic risks include economic, environmental, political, social, and technological risks. Microeconomic risks include concentrations of vendors or customers, fraudulent reporting, inefficiency, and employee theft.

Most macroeconomic risks and many microeconomic risks fall purely under the purview of enterprise risk management and, if the board has a designated risk committee, likely fall outside the scope of work of the audit committee. What all audit committees must focus on are those microeconomic risks related to fraud that, as defined by the PCAOB, could provide opportunities for the "company's internal control over financial reporting [to] fail to prevent or detect misstatement caused by fraud."[3]

The board's role in risk management is oversight. If an organization has a risk committee, that committee is charged with this responsibility. If no risk committee has been impaneled, the duties of risk management could fall upon the audit committee or board.

The goal of risk identification is to consider all possible risks without regard to their likelihood or severity. Such judgments come later in the risk-management process. Rather, during the risk-identification phase, the purpose of risk management is to identify as large a pool of risks as possible. Organizations may vary in their methods of identifying risks, though many choose to start with either interviews or surveys. Organizations must decide whom to include in the risk-identification process; some organizations select just a few senior executives, while other organizations opt to distribute surveys or conduct interviews more widely throughout the organization.

In developing survey or interview questions, a variety of leading questions can be posed to promote conversation, including:

> What fraud losses have been suffered in the past?
> What fraud losses keep you up at night?
> What new fraud schemes are possible due to changes in technology or business structure?
> What fraud risks are regulated?
> What could go wrong?
> What must go right for us to succeed?

ACTION STEPS

▲ Understand the types of macro- and microeconomic risks that may affect your organization.

▲ Learn how to recognize microeconomic risks related to fraud that could provide opportunities to fail to prevent or detect fraud.

▲ Adopt a risk-management framework that ponders risks, both known and unforeseen.

Risk-Ranking Tools

Once the universe of fraud risks for an organization is identified, those risks must be ranked so that focus can be directed for efficiency and effectiveness. The two basic methodologies for ranking risk can be described as either statistical or judgment-based. Both methods develop a composite risk score based on the likelihood that a risk will occur and the value of the loss if such a risk occurs. The composite risk score can be written as a formula:

Composite risk score = Likelihood x Severity

Statistical Risk Ranking

Statistical risk ranking relies on historical data to define the frequency and severity of loss for various risks. Although most organizations do not have enough of this data, insurance companies and other aggregators of enormous databases of losses are well positioned to use a statistic-based risk-ranking model to prioritize risk. The statistical risk-ranking methodology utilizes a weighted average approach, taking into account the likelihood of a loss (measured in percentage) and severity of the loss (measured in dollar value) if such a loss occurs.

So if an organization identified a set of risks—such as risk of cash-register embezzlement, purchasing-agent kickbacks, and financial statement earnings restatement—those risks could be expressed statistically as:

Risk of cash-register embezzlement
Risk = Likelihood x Severity
= 11.8% x $20,000[4]
= $2,360

Risk of purchasing-agent kickback (collusion)
Risk = Likelihood x Severity
= 5.7% x $200,000[5]
= $11,400

Risk of financial statement earnings restatement
Risk = Likelihood x Severity
= 7.6% x $1,000,000[6]
= $76,000

To rank these risks using a statistical risk-ranking model, the risks would be prioritized as:

Rank	Risk ($)	Risk
1	76,000	Financial Statement Earnings Restatement
2	11,400	Purchasing-Agent Kickbacks (Collusion)
3	2,360	Cash-Register Embezzlement

In the lens of the statistical risk-ranking method for this example, the highest risk for the audit committee to consider would be the risk of a financial statement earnings restatement, followed by purchasing-agent kickbacks and, least of all, cash-register embezzlement schemes.

Judgment-Based Risk Ranking

Organizations that lack sufficient historical data find that the statistically based risk-ranking model is imprecise, and so applying it could lead to errors in risk prioritization. In the absence of sufficient statistical data to inform risk ranking, many organizations must rely on a judgment-based risk-ranking methodology. Organizations still evaluate the likelihood and severity of the risk, but instead of percentages and dollar amounts, risk is described as either low/middle/high or on a numerical scale with a range of 1 to 3 or 1 to 5.

Despite the lack of concrete data, a judgment-based risk-ranking process is, in most cases, the best way of developing a composite risk score because most organizations lack sufficient data to use a statistical-based risk-ranking model. Skeptics of judgment-based risk ranking may discredit results as capricious guesses made on the part of risk managers. Therefore, acknowledging the limitations of the judgment-based risk-ranking methodology may go a long way toward improving adoption of the overall risk-assessment process.

In using this method, risk managers must assign a value of both the likelihood and the severity of risk based on their own judgment as well as the judgment of the risk-assessment team entrusted with providing input. The use of a number scale with the top value being either 3 or 5, rather than a low/middle/high scale, allows for organizations to arrive at a composite risk that has a number value that can be ranked from highest to lowest. While the judgment-based risk-ranking methodology that involves rating likelihood and severity as low/middle/high does allow for ranking, the output of such a process does not lend itself well to ordinal ranking, which may be easier to communicate across the organization.

Under a judgment-based risk-ranking methodology, the same risks evaluated under the statistical-based risk-ranking methodology demonstrated above could be expressed on a scale of 1 to 3:

Risk of cash-register embezzlement
Risk = Likelihood x Severity
= 1 x 1
= 1

Risk of purchasing-agent kickback (collusion)
Risk = Likelihood x Severity
= 2 x 2
= 4

Risk of financial statement earnings restatement
Risk = Likelihood x Severity
= 2 x 3
= 6

To rank these risks using a judgment-based ranking model, the risks would be prioritized with the highest scores ranked as most severe. Given the value range of the two dimensions of risk of likelihood and severity of 1 to 3, the minimum risk score would be 1 and the maximum risk score would be 9.

Rank	Risk Score	Risk
1	6	Financial Statement Earnings Restatement
2	4	Purchasing-Agent Kickbacks (Collusion)
3	1	Cash-Register Embezzlement

Risk Velocity

In addition to the two dimensions of composite risk of likelihood and severity, there is also some discussion among lead risk-management practitioners of risk velocity. Risk velocity attempts to describe the severity of a risk based on how quickly things can go badly, as well as how well the effectiveness of mitigating controls can minimize these short-fused risks.

To illustrate the impact of risk velocity, consider the public relations disasters that often follow public reporting of a fraud or other risk events. As noted in the COSO report *Fraudulent Financial Reporting: 1998–2007—An Analysis of U.S. Public Companies*, the announcement of fraud led to a 16.7 percent decrease in stock price on the day of and the day after the announcement,[7] and so risk velocity of a reported fraud would be high.

In the case of the 2010 BP Deepwater Horizon oil spill in the Gulf of Mexico, it's easy to see how the occurrence of a risk event can be tremendously damaging within just a short period of time. For example, just before the disaster, BP's stock was trading at $59. When the oil rig exploded in April 2010, killing 11 workers and leading to the largest offshore oil spill in U.S. history, BP's stock price plummeted, reaching a nadir of $27 in June 2010, its lowest price in more than a decade. BP scrambled for weeks to try to resolve the problem.

The presence of a well-designed and executed crisis media-management plan can reduce the risk velocity (i.e., the acceleration of bad publicity that can follow) of the announcement of an environmental hazard or other disaster (see Chapter 10). Organizations that possess a strong crisis media plan are likely to suffer fewer ill effects of risk velocity. Hence, consideration of risk velocity has become more popular as audit committees and other board committees attempt to use the risk-assessment process to focus efforts on those risks that are most likely to endanger organizational goals.

ACTION STEPS

▲ Learn how to rank risk so that focus can be directed for efficiency and effectiveness.

▲ Learn the differences and benefits of statistical risk ranking and judgment-based risk ranking and how those methods can help determine the likelihood that a risk will occur and the value of the loss if such a risk occurs.

▲ Select a risk-ranking method that matches the organization's quality of data, with only those organizations with rich databases of historical losses likely to select a statistically based model, while the rest rely on judgment-based risk-ranking methodologies.

Risk Response

The effort of arriving at a composite risk score only gets risk managers part of the way in determining how to treat risk. Risk managers cannot prudently turn away from every risk, because some risks may be worth taking based on the promised return. While every opportunity comes with a certain degree of risk, there is, unfortunately, not always a direct correlation between risk and reward. Some activities can be high return and low risk. Other activities may be low return and high risk. The job of risk management is to determine which opportunities are worth the attendant risk.

Once risks are identified and ranked based on likelihood and severity, the risk-management team is ready to treat risk. A meaningful first step in risk treatment is defining the organization's risk appetite. Organizations that treat risk at varying levels of responsibility will likely find that risk appetites differ at the various levels within an organization, with lower levels of management typically more sensitive to relatively low-dollar value losses than higher level management. For example, a $100,000 loss could be catastrophic to a line manager but tolerable at the CEO level.

Defining Risk Appetite

How much risk an organization is willing to take on in pursuit of a hoped-for promised outcome must be examined and articulated as part of the audit committee's pursuit of responsible governance. The level of appropriate risk appetite is determined by management and approved by the audit committee. For those resistant to embracing risk management, it can be helpful to consider that risk treatment can, at times, embolden organizations to take on additional risk once risks are understood and evaluated to be within acceptable risk tolerances.

To aid in defining an organization's risk appetite, COSO has presented a set of questions "to solicit the viewpoints of senior executives and board members on the appropriate risk levels for the entity. For example:

- Do shareholders want us to pursue high risk/high return businesses, or do they prefer a more conservative, predictable business profile?
- What is our desired credit rating?
- What is our desired confidence level for paying dividends?
- How much of our budget can we subject to potential loss?
- How much earnings volatility are we prepared to accept?
- Are there specific risks we are not prepared to accept?
- What is our willingness to consider growth through acquisitions?
- What is our willingness to experience damage to our reputation or brand?

- To what extent are we willing to expand our product, customer, or geographic coverage?

- What amount of risk are we willing to accept on new initiatives to achieve a specified target (e.g., 15% return on investment)?"[8]

As noted in the varying points of focus in the questions above, risk appetite may be qualitative (in terms of risks of compliance violations or reputational loss) or quantitative (in terms of dollar loss or credit ratings). The key with effective definition of risk appetite is in being as specific as possible as to the conditions, both economic and qualitative, that satisfy an organization's risk tolerances. Once risk appetite has been articulated, risk managers are ready to treat risk by deciding whether to accept, share, mitigate, or avoid the risk.

Accepting Risk

Organizations may choose to retain some known risks without much thought. These may be risks that present only a minor disruption to operations or threaten a loss deemed insignificant to overall organizational objectives. In the risk-ranking discussion above, for example, the threat of cash-register embezzlement, as irritating as it is, may pose such a minor risk to the organization that it, at least at the board level, may deem further study unnecessary.

It should be noted that the decision to accept a risk at the board level does not mean that the fraud risk is insignificant at the senior or line-manager level. This highlights the importance of defining risk appetites at different organizational levels. An expected loss of $20,000 from cash-register embezzlement may be immaterial to the board of directors and perhaps even senior management. However, the loss of $20,000 from cash-register embezzlement could pose a significant drain on a retail outlet and, as such, may be deemed a significant risk to the store manager.

Sharing Risk

The risk-management team decides whether to share risk, and organizations that choose to share risk with third parties typically do so through joint ventures or insurance. Risks shared through joint ventures allow organizations to share risk and rewards in accordance to percentages specified in a joint-venture agreement.

Insurance products also allow organizations to share risk but offer more ways than most joint-venture arrangements to apportion risk and reward. Some insurance products offer risk sharing based on defined percentages, as is the case with coinsurance for health coverage. Other insurance products allow organizations to divest of all risk for losses above specified dollar amounts, as with high-dollar deductible health insurance plans. Still other insurance products offer combinations of risk sharing and risk divestiture, allowing organizations be highly selective in the risks retained.

Because the cost of insurance reduces returns, either through the need to pay a set fee or by sharing a percentage of returns or losses, it is not always in the best interest of organizations to reduce the risks retained much below risk tolerances. Risk sharing may be done in conjunction with risk acceptance, if the risk retained after insurance brings the remaining risk within risk tolerances. Or it can be done in conjunction with risk mitigation, especially in instances in which the conditions of insurance underwriting prescribe specific actions by the organization.

Mitigating Risk

As with the choice to reduce risk and level of risk appetite, the choice to mitigate risk is made by the risk-management team and approved by the audit committee as part of the overall oversight role the audit committee performs over risk management. Risks treated through mitigation are those risks whose risk ratings can be reduced through the effective implementation of controls. The ability of the risk rating for an activity to decline in the presence of effective controls highlights the difference between inherent and residual risk.

Inherent risk is the level of risk that exists because of the nature of the activity. For example, inherent risks exist anytime there are cash receipts for an operation. Therefore, the inherent risk for a cash-based business would be high. Residual risk quantifies the risk that remains once controls are in place. So, with the case of a cash-based business, the risk of cash-register theft can be reduced if controls such as video surveillance and manager approval of void sales are in place. Accordingly, the effective operation of such controls would allow the residual risk to be much lower than the inherent risk.

In consideration of risk treatment, those activities with an inherent risk above stated risk tolerances either must have mitigating controls that bring residual risk within stated tolerances, or the risk must be avoided. So, for example, in the case of cash-register embezzlement, the likely loss is $20,000. For organizations with a stated risk tolerance of $15,000, mitigating controls would have to be implemented to retain the risk.

Mitigating controls may already be in place, or new procedures may need to be designed to bring residual risks within stated tolerances. An essential component of effective risk management is ensuring that the identified mitigating controls are operating effectively.

Avoiding Risk

There are some opportunities with such a high level of risk that organizations may choose to avoid those activities as part of prudent governance. In other cases, while the inherent risk could be mitigated to reduce the residual risk to a tolerable level, the expense of the mitigating controls could exceed the promised return of the activity. At other times, the mitigating controls could fail to bring the residual risk down sufficiently for the level of risk appetite defined for that particular organization.

For example, with the cost of effective compliance with SOX estimated at $2.5 million a year,[9] some organizations may choose to avoid registering as a public company. For organizations considering competing in the global marketplace, concerns over the cost of effectively implementing a Foreign Corrupt Practices Act compliance program may prompt organizations to limit the amount of trade they do with countries perceived to have high corruption.

ACTION STEPS

▲ Discuss and define risk appetites, being as specific as possible about the qualitative and quantitative standards allowable to ensure appropriate response when business conditions change.

▲ Determine how much risk the organization is willing to take on in pursuit of anticipated outcomes.

▲ Determine acceptable risks at all levels of the organization.

▲ Consider whether sharing risk with third parties is appropriate and, if so, to what extent sharing risk may be practical.

Reporting Risk

The energy spent assessing risk would be lost if the significant risks identified were not brought to the full attention of those capable of mitigating losses. So once risks are identified and prioritized, risk-management efforts must transition to communicating those risks to those in governance and, perhaps, to team members.

Most publicly traded companies include a list of significant risks in their 10-K filings. Public or private, many organizations choose to include in their board reports a listing of significant risks. While these methods rely primarily on verbal descriptions of risks, visual methods of expressing risk exist that have the ability to clearly and quickly highlight those risks most worthy of oversight.

A leading visual method for reporting risks is heat mapping. Heat maps are prepared by the risk-management team and reviewed by the board. When used to report risk, they typically are displayed as quadrant graphs calibrating loss from low to high, with the two dimensions being likelihood of loss and severity of loss. Figure 8.1 illustrates a heat map that reports the three risks evaluated in the risk-ranking discussion above.

The heat map for reporting risks consists of three color bands: green, yellow, and red. For the purposes of this illustration, band 1 would be red, band 2 would be yellow, and band 3 would be green.

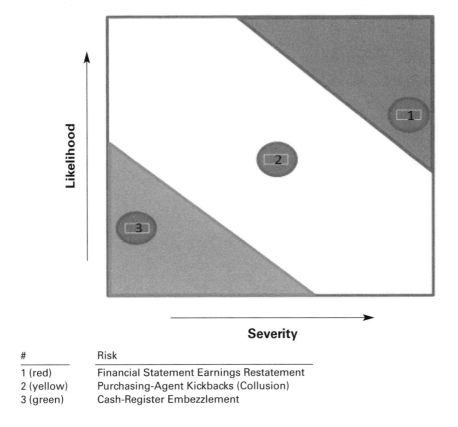

#	Risk
1 (red)	Financial Statement Earnings Restatement
2 (yellow)	Purchasing-Agent Kickbacks (Collusion)
3 (green)	Cash-Register Embezzlement

Figure 8.1   Heat map, inherent risks displayed.

The green band indicates those risks that fall within specific risk tolerances. Activities with a composite risk that fall in the yellow band would indicate a risk that should be watched and most likely retained either through risk sharing or risk mitigation. Those risks that fall within the red band represent risks so severe that they should either be avoided or, at the very least, mitigated and shared if such efforts can bring residual risk within stated risk tolerances.

In the risk-ranking discussion above, three risks were considered: cash-register embezzlement, purchasing-agent kickbacks, and financial statement earnings restatements. Each of these risks has mitigating controls that can be applied in order to reduce the inherent risk. Video surveillance and managerial approval of voids, for example, can be used as mitigating controls for cash-register embezzlement. (See Chapter 9 for a discussion on mitigating controls that can be used to reduce the risks of kickbacks and earnings restatements.)

In discussions of risk response, evaluation of residual risk is often more informative than consideration of inherent risk. Risk managers can express risk by mapping residual risk alone, as seen in Figure 8.1, or they can show the transition of risk from inherent to residual, as shown in Figure 8.2. Demonstrating the transition of risk from inherent to residual can be particularly influential when risk managers are hoping to secure the necessary resources to implement mitigating controls.

Audit committee and board members are likely to see more

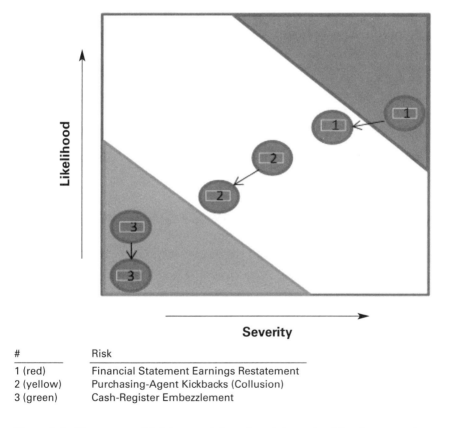

#	Risk
1 (red)	Financial Statement Earnings Restatement
2 (yellow)	Purchasing-Agent Kickbacks (Collusion)
3 (green)	Cash-Register Embezzlement

Figure 8.2   Heat map, with inherent risks reduced through mitigating controls.

risks populated on a heat map than just the three illustrated in these examples. Many boards like to see 10 to 15 risk events illustrated in a heat map. The placement of various activities in the different color bands is most likely determined from judgment-based risk ranking. Therefore, audit committee and board members should be invited to discuss the placement of risk for the various activities within the different color bands to verify the soundness of the reasoning made by the risk managers in assigning the composite risk scores.

Another aspect of heat mapping that organizations can leverage is the use of heat mapping by team members. While the risks deemed significant to audit committee and board members may be at a larger scale than they would be to business-unit and line managers, each level of management has its own set of risks that needs to be monitored. Therefore, organizations should consider extending the use of heat mapping beyond board reporting. Those organizations that utilize process-improvement and quality-management initiatives to report business-unit and division-level goals and results are well positioned to add heat mapping of risks to the set of reports posted in common areas.

One final consideration for audit committees and boards in the use of heat mapping is the method of reporting risks for various divisions and business units. Some organizations may choose to report risks for all divisions on one organization-level quadrant heat map, while other organizations may choose to report risks on different quadrant graphs for each division. Yet another way to present risks for different divisions is by using a bull's-eye heat map.

A bull's-eye heat map still displays risks, with green being the inner ring and red being the outer ring, to illustrate the low-to-high risks. However, bull's-eye heat mapping expresses the risk for different business segments or divisions, as its own area in the bull's-eye graph. In Figure 8.3, three divisions of an organization have the risks for that particular division displayed. As is evident from the concentration of risks displayed for each division, division C has more high-level risks than divisions A and B. While it is at the discretion of the board to

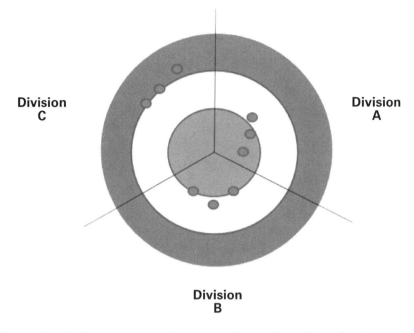

Figure 8.3   Bull's-eye heat map, for organizations with multiple divisions.

decide if the returns from division C merit the additional risk exposure, the use of bull's-eye heat mapping does highlight those divisions with the greatest risk exposure. Bull's-eye heat mapping should be considered at the board level for organizations with multiple divisions.

ACTION STEPS

⚠ Ensure that risk-management efforts are communicated to governance officers and team members as appropriate.

⚠ Ensure that each level of management is monitoring and reporting on its own set of risks.

⚠ Take advantage of visual risk reporting where possible, including heat mapping and compliance testing results.

Risk-Assessment Follow-Up

If all they consist of are discussions within the risk-management team, risk-management efforts ultimately fail to deliver the full promise that the proactive risk treatment of risk management implies. To maximize the benefits, organizations must integrate risk awareness into the areas of strategic planning, ethics-policy development, internal controls design, and compliance testing.

Strategic Planning

Perhaps one of the most powerful outcomes of risk management is the benefit to strategic management when risks are known and addressed so that organizations don't suffer from the drama of unexpected surprises. Uncontained risk can quickly erode any gains, as seen with the collapse of Lehman Brothers in 2008. Lehman, which was forced to liquidate after suffering huge losses in the mortgage market, saw its stock price plummet and investor confidence erode after the risks of long-term assets backing overnight lending were not given appropriate weight by those in governance when considering the sustainability of Lehman's business model of pooling mortgage-backed securities for resale.

Risk management must occupy space in strategic planning because risk response affects organizational goals. In a perfect world, risks are understood and retained only if residual risks fall within agreed-upon risk appetites. For those risks where residual risk do not meet stated risk tolerances, despite best efforts to share or mitigate risk, those in governance must avoid such risks. These instances in which appealing opportunities must be refused because of poor risk-reward trade-offs demonstrate one of the most fundamental roles of those in governance who are commanded to be responsible stewards of organizational resources.

Risk treatment that includes risk sharing and risk mitigation must also include strategic planning that articulates benchmarks and contingency plans for failure of prescribed mitigating controls. Audit committee members are responsible for overseeing the risk-management team's efforts in this matter. In addition, strategic planning must have a ready response for exiting risky activities once the residual risk falls outside of agreed-upon risk tolerances.

For example, for risk-sharing arrangements that include insurance, the sustainability of an insurance carrier must be monitored because the failure of the insurance company would imply any losses must be absorbed by the organization. If the insurance company's health declines, as evidenced by industry ratings, an organization relying on risk sharing should have backup plans as part of its strategic plans to either secure alternate insurance coverage or divest itself of the risky activity. Plans to retain risk based on risk sharing and mitigation that lack benchmarks and contingency plans could leave an organization in no better position than had the organization not done any risk planning whatsoever.

Managing Real-World Risk

Of course, no one wants to be the naysayer of the group. Nonetheless, those in governance who are committed to being good stewards of resources can often be put in the position of highlighting the negatives in a situation in an effort to preserve organizational resources. To assist those pressed into service as the person to say no, some sound business principles can bolster the credibility of those on a campaign to retreat. Examples of well-respected business philosophies that promote curtailing business opportunities include those of Jim Collins, Peter Drucker, and Donald Trump.

In *Good to Great*, Jim Collins suggests that companies focus only on those business activities at which the organization excels, cutting out business activities at which the organization performs just so-so.[10] Such advice can embolden risk managers to focus compliance efforts on primary lines of business, rather than scatter compliance efforts among disparate risk sources.

Peter Drucker instructs in *The Daily Drucker* that organizations stop squandering resources on obsolete businesses. Drucker believes that identifying and terminating obsolete businesses frees up valuable financial and human resources to more productive uses. Drucker states that "nothing is as futile as trying to keep a corpse from stinking," and he notes that many organizations try hard to ignore dwindling businesses and that their futile efforts always fail in the end, after incurring unnecessary losses.[11]

Donald Trump adds his own advice on the wisdom of playing devil's advocate when he points out the wisdom of asking "What am I pretending not to see?" in his book *Never Give Up*.[12] Such wisdom is hard earned for Trump, who, in the fullness of the highs and lows in his career, has suffered significant losses when only the most optimistic projections were taken into account in strategic decisions. Trump's question on pondering the existence of unknown risks serves as a basis for the risk-identification phase of risk management.

These well-respected business principles can help risk managers and audit committee and board members who are suggesting an organization discontinue business activities carrying higher risks that do not align with the organization's primary business strengths.

Ethics-Policy Development

Audit committee members are responsible for oversight of ethics-policy development. The development of an ethics policy should include the recommendation to enhance standard ethics policies by addressing specific risks for an organization identified as part of the risk-management program. The need to include targeted provisions to address organization-specific risks may require an organization to go beyond boilerplate ethics policies to truly equip team members to identify and resist likely fraud scenarios.

For example, organizations whose business requires a great deal of travel can expand the section of expense reimbursements to include specific scenarios for purchases eligible for repayment. Organizations with exposure to related-party-transaction and conflicts-of-interest risks would do well to go beyond stating edicts for business integrity and provide examples of business relationships that do, and perhaps more importantly do not, pass the smell test. Such clarifications using scenario discussions reduce confusion on the part of the team, improving ethics standards while at the same time taking away the so-called stupidity defense asserted by those who claim they didn't know any better.

Internal Controls Design

Audit committee members play a key role in the oversight of integrating mitigating controls into the internal controls design. For those risks retained only in the presence of mitigating controls, the integration of mitigating controls into the internal controls design is an essential step in reducing a business activity's inherent risk to an acceptable level of residual risk.

For example, if an organization is subject to a high risk of doing business with shell companies, the performance of internal control procedures of vendor due diligence and compliance testing can be included to reduce the inherent risk to a tolerable level of residual risk. Such prescribed controls, if necessary to bring residual risks down within stated risk appetite, should be added to an organization's standard operating procedures.

Compliance Testing

For some business activities, the effective operation of a key mitigating control is the only thing reducing inherent risk to an acceptable residual risk. In such cases, the testing of key mitigating controls is a necessary component of effective risk management. The audit committee should communicate with those performing the internal audit function to ensure that the key mitigating controls identified in the risk-response phase are tested periodically, and that instances of noncompliance are reported to the audit committee. While such communications between those performing the internal audit function and the audit committee may be done only verbally, some organizations choose to document the findings of compliance testing on key mitigating controls. There is no standard manner of communicating compliance findings.

Figure 8.4 illustrates a visual method for communicating the results of compliance testing. Each row contains a key mitigating control. Each column reflects the results of compliance testing for each month of the year. Figure 8.4 uses light to dark shading to graphically illustrate the failure or success of various mitigating controls. Some organizations may use numbers or letters to indicate the results of compliance testing. As evidenced in the row presenting compliance results for supervisory review of credit memos issued, several months of noncompliance were followed by a significant breach. Such a pattern of noncompliance followed by a significant breach is common. This can happen because a potential fraudster may notice a control weakness by mistake, and then, when the mistake is not detected, be emboldened to take advantage of the apparent opportunity. Therefore, noncompliance, even without serious breaches, should be taken seriously by those in governance.

Mitigating Control	J	F	M	A	M	J	J	A	S	O	N	D
Monthly Statements to Customers												
Reconciling Shipping Tickets to Invoices												
Supervisory Approval of Sales Discount												
Supervisory Review of Credit Memos Issued												
Continuous Monitoring of Expense Reports												
Time Card Audits												
Matching Invoices to Receiving Slip and P.O.												
Vendor Evaluation Process												

☐ Control operating consistently and effectively.

☐ Control operating effectively a majority of the time. No significant breaches noted.

■ Control NOT operating consistently. Significant breaches noted.

Figure 8.4 Compliance chart, reporting compliance for various key mitigating controls.

ACTION STEPS

⚠ Pull through risk awareness into strategic planning, being bold to advise rejection of business activities that do not conform to stated risk tolerances.

⚠ Have contingency plans to exit risky business activities when conditions push residual risks outside risk tolerances.

⚠ Make the ethics policy come alive with discussion of scenarios that illustrate sensitive business situations prone to fraud risks.

⚠ Communicate with those performing the internal audit function to be sure that key mitigating controls identified are operating effectively.

CHAPTER NINE

Spearhead Fraud-Deterrence Initiatives

FRAUD, WITH LOSSES estimated at 5 percent of Gross World Product,[1] is a scourge on economic development that cannot be ignored. The Association of Certified Fraud Examiners (ACFE) has amassed enormous amounts of data about the effectiveness of various fraud-deterrence tools and has found that many of the least expensive ones, such as hotlines and employee training, are the most effective.

There's nothing new about occupational fraud. Modern technology may have changed how people steal, but the motives and the classifications of fraud schemes remain unchanged. What also has changed is the level of accountability for fraud deterrence expected of board directors and, specifically, audit committee members.

Aside from being responsible for the loss of dollars due to fraud, board and audit committee members must also counter the indirect costs of fraud. COSO issued a report in 2010 regarding losses related to fraudulent financial statements, noting that stocks dropped 16.7 percent within two days of an earnings restatement. The COSO report also noted that of the 347 victim organizations examined, the cumulative misstatements amounted to $120 billion, placing fraud deterrence as an essential responsibility for board directors who serve as stewards of organizational resources.[2]

In this chapter we identify the most commonly practiced types of fraud and then outline the most effective fraud-deterrence tools available that organizations can implement, regardless of organizational size.

Types of Fraud

There are three commonly accepted types of fraud, as illustrated in the Association of Certified Fraud Examiners' fraud tree: corruption, asset misappropriation, and fraudulent statements (see Figure 9.1). Each fraud type has its own frequency and severity, with asset misap-

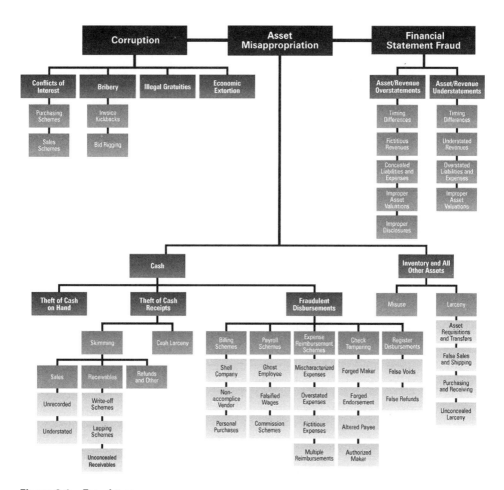

Figure 9.1   Fraud tree.
Source: Association of Certified Fraud Examiners

propriation being the most common but least costly and fraudulent statements being the least likely but most costly.

Corruption

The ACFE reports that corruption occurs in 33 percent of fraud cases reported and that the median loss is $250,000.[3] Corruption, which comes in a variety of types, most often includes conflicts of interest and bribery. Like other types of frauds, corruption percolates when those placed in a position of trust put their own individual interests ahead of organizational goals.

Conflicts of Interest

The nature of capitalism demands that there are times when the advantage of one stakeholder comes at the expense of another. In regard to executive compensation, shareholders wish to keep compensation low, while managers wish to maximize their paychecks; managers and employees work at cross-purposes over employee wages; and customers and companies often have differing views about predatory pricing and product-safety concerns. Conflicts of interest among the various stakeholders of an organization serve as a potent breeding ground for corruption schemes.

Few organizations illustrate the dangers of conflicts of interest as well as AIG. Years before the financial collapse, back in 2002, *Businessweek* called out AIG as an organization with atrocious corporate governance. Per *Businessweek*, AIG Chairman and CEO Maurice R. "Hank" Greenberg controlled and ran two private companies that had substantial business dealings with AIG, with one of the related parties operating as "a veritable bank vault, paying out tens of millions in cash and stock to AIG executives outside the purview of the board's compensation committee."[4] By 2010, AIG had failed, receiving a $182 billion bailout, the largest corporate bailout in history. Much of AIG's failure has been traced back to conflicts of interest, delusion, and deception.

Individuals who serve within organizations are trusted to act in the best interest of those organizations. However, there are times when personal stakes compete with organizational goals, creating conflicts of interest that may result in personal enrichment for the individual at the expense of the organization and its shareholders. Particularly frequent areas in which conflicts of interest surface include related-party transactions, executive compensation, and insider trading.

Related-Party Transactions Related-party transactions tend to step over the line when trade terms with a related-party entity do not meet market conditions, which may lead to an organization paying higher prices or receiving inferior goods. Related-party transactions do occur, and when arms-length terms can be proven to exist, many organizations permit related-party transactions. A transaction carried out with arms-length terms indicates that the business terms of the contract, such as payment amounts and collection periods, are similar to the terms that would have been agreed upon by unrelated parties. Some organizations may even find that they pay less for goods or services under such terms than they would have to pay a third party.

Disclosing related-party transactions is a regulatory requirement of directors and officers of publicly traded companies, and is included in the code of conduct of many private organizations. The difficulty for board directors and audit committee members in trying to limit corruption stemming from related-party transactions is that related-party status may, in many cases, be difficult to discern unless it is specifically disclosed. Yet appropriate monitoring of related-party transactions to ensure that such close relations with trade partners does not lead to corruption relies heavily on self-disclosure. Special attention should be paid to related-party transactions in which the related parties are audited by a firm other than one's own auditing firm or are not audited at all.

A common related-party transaction involves the exchange of money to company officers for services that were either unapproved or fictitious, as is the case of sales through employees who approve their own invoices, or a shell company operated by an employee. At the highest levels of management, this practice of approving fictitious sales can be very expensive.[5] A 2011 case with Pamrapo Service Corp., a New Jersey–based investment company, erupted when a senior manager set up a scheme that allowed him to embezzle more than $571,000 in commissions and fees. The commission scheme was considered fraudulent because it was approved by a related party, his father, in the counter-party organization, No one else in either organization was aware of the arrangement.[6]

Another frequent type of related-party transactions involves loans to related parties. For example, Pennsylvania-based cable-television company Adelphia Communications suffered dearly for fraudulently excluding billions of dollars in liabilities from the balance sheets by hiding them in off-balance sheet affiliates and inflating earnings. Adelphia compounded its governance woes when the board allowed for rampant self-dealing by the Rigas family, which had founded the company.[7] Much to the regret of the shareholders and other stakeholders of Adelphia, the board allowed the Rigas family to borrow more than $230 million.[8] John Rigas was forced to resign as CEO in 2002 after being indicted for bank fraud, wire fraud, and securities fraud; two of his sons also were charged in the matter. Reports note that the Rigas family borrowed $3.1 billion from Adelphia without disclosing the loans. Adelphia was forced to file for bankruptcy.

Nowadays, direct loans to executives have ceased because they are specifically banned under SOX.

ACTION STEPS

A Set a clear policy on what represents a related party, including examples.

A Request staff to self-report related parties annually.

A Perform independent investigation of related-party disclosures, with ongoing monitoring for approved related-party transactions.

Executive Compensation Perhaps no area of conflict of interest provides as much leeway for abuse as executive compensation. The divergence between individual self-interest and organizational goals is at its height when senior executives negotiate the value of their contribution to the organization, made evident by the sight of so many executives receiving generous compensation despite poor business performance. Notable instances of lavish executive pay include AMR Corp., which paid CEO Gerard Arpey $5.2 million in total compensation in 2010, even though the parent company of American Airlines was the only major U.S. carrier to lose money that year[9]; Manulife, which paid its CEO $9.3 million despite a 2010 net loss[10]; and Time Warner, which increased 2010 pay to its executives despite revenue losses.[11]

Despite the effect of generous executive compensation on diminished shareholder returns, rewarding executives for high performance is the cornerstone of our capitalist system. Executive compensation arrangements that have performance-based components work to align personal goals with organizational success.

Finding the right balance in sharing organizational profits between shareholders and executives can be tricky. Pay multiplier, which reports the ratio of wages of the highest and lowest compensated individuals in an organization, illustrates the growing divergence in pay between top management and the rank-and-file. Executive compensation levels have become so absurd that recent pay multipliers fall in the range of 400 to 1[12] to 800 to 1.[13] Compare that to the pay multiplier during the at-the-time considered greedy 1980s of 42 to 1. Yet to look at the other end of the spectrum, some organizations have found that efforts to curtail extravagant executive compensation can work against organizational success. For example, during the 1980s, Ben and Jerry's ice cream company embraced a rule that limited the pay multiplier to 7 to 1,[14] only to end this practice in 1994 because the company suffered from high CEO turnover and substandard performance.

The ability of performance-based pay to help align executive interests with organizational success cannot be ignored. But board members must take measures to set appropriate limits on senior executive pay multipliers that honor the economic logic of capitalism while not allowing senior executives to take the lion's share of economic rewards.

ACTION STEPS

▲ Form an independent compensation committee.

▲ Remain conscientious in connecting performance with pay, incorporating long-term strategic goals and other shareholder interests.

▲ Allow shareholder input on executive compensation decisions by offering "say on pay" proxies on shareholder ballots.

Insider Trading Trading securities of one's own firm based on nonpublic information—that is, insider trading—is considered fraudulent, with the United States and several other nations requiring disclosure of any trading in the organization's stock by key employees. Trading on nonpublic information violates the implicit agreement that employees will act in the best interest of shareholders. To discourage insider trading, many organizations prohibit it as part of the employee code of ethics.

Although audit committee members may not be responsible for directly detecting or preventing insider trading, they need to be aware of the potential for it, ensuring both that they monitor executives, managers, and staff for any potential insider trading and that they themselves do not reveal information to outsiders that could be construed as insider information.

Bribery

In addition to conflicts of interest, bribery is another type of corruption of which board directors and audit committee members must be aware and against which they must be vigilant. Bribery schemes can involve either the supply or demand side. Supplying bribes to foreign officials is prohibited under the Foreign Corrupt Practices Act (see Chapter 7). The demand side of bribery occurs when an organization's employee receives a bribe in exchange for a favor that injures shareholders, because the favor typically involves an organization paying for nonexistent, inferior, or overpriced goods or services.

Bribes, also known as kickbacks, can come in the form of cash, trips, or any economic consideration given to employees that results in the company receiving poor quality goods, paying inflated prices, or receiving below-market revenues on sales. Purchasing managers have been known to receive not only cash, but everything from free carpet cleaning to new driveways to professional landscaping services.

Typical bribery schemes with vendors involve kickbacks to secure contracts either in a no-bid environment, bid-rigging, or payment of bogus invoices. Bribery schemes with customers can result in unauthorized discounts or credit memos that allow third parties to pocket organizational proceeds undetected.

At the board level, the first line of defense is a clearly defined gift policy. Aside from that, board and audit committee members can look for other red flags of kickbacks that may include, as listed in W. Steve Albrecht and Chad O. Albrecht's book, *Fraud Examination and Prevention:*

> ➤ Decreasing quality of goods received, which would be noticed either as a quality control problem upon receipt, as a production delay that resulted from abnormally high defect rates, or through higher-than-average customer returns.

> ➤ Decreasing purchases from other vendors or increasing purchases from favored vendor. To catch this trend, it's a good idea to compare the top 10 vendors from one year to the next.

> ➤ Increasing prices. Ask the purchasing manager about parts that have experienced price increases greater than 10 percent (or whatever percentage increase makes sense for the company or industry).

> ➤ A purchasing agent having a nicer automobile or home than would be expected, and other indications that the agent is living beyond his or her means. Put another way, perform a "lifestyle audit" in order to ensure that living standards are in line with reported income.[15]

Kickback schemes can also be discovered through complaints filed by unsuccessful bidders for company contracts. Unsuccessful bidders are very willing to report competitors who seem to be getting contracts using inferior goods or inflated prices. To catch kickback schemes through feedback from unsuccessful bidders, organizations should include information regarding the organization's whistle-blower hotline on purchase orders and requests for proposals.

ACTION STEPS

▲ Set a clear policy on allowable gifts.

▲ Increase scrutiny on those who have the ability to award contracts.

▲ Perform lifestyle audits.

▲ Offer a whistle-blower hotline.

Asset Misappropriation

Asset misappropriation represents the most frequent type of fraud, according to the ACFE 2012 *Report to the Nations on Occupational Fraud and Abuse*, with a frequency of 86.7 percent (see Figure 9.2). Fraud through asset misappropriation can involve the theft of cash, inventory, fixed assets, or even intellectual property. While cash is easier to convert into value than other assets subject to theft, non-cash misappropriations represent a significant portion of asset-misappropriation cases, 17.2 percent of cases according to the ACFE 2012 *Report to the Nations*.[16]

The three leading types of asset-misappropriation schemes, in order of relative expensiveness, are two cash-based schemes—billing and check tampering—and noncash asset misappropriation. These three types account for more than half of all asset-misappropriation schemes reported.

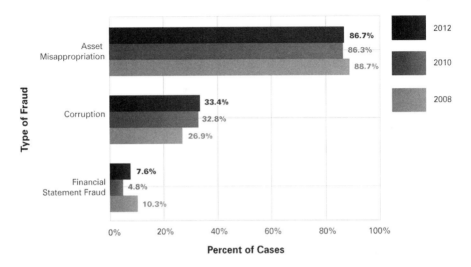

Figure 9.2 Frequency of fraud by type.
Source: ACFE 2012 Report to the Nations on Occupational Fraud and Abuse

Billing and Check-Tampering Schemes

Board directors and audit committee members need to be aware of various tampering schemes that could have detrimental effects on the organization. The two leading cash-based asset-misappropriation schemes involve billing and check tampering. Billing schemes operate through the cash-disbursement process by circumventing controls so that the organization pays for either nonexistent, inferior, or over-priced goods and services. In the case of check tampering, the cash disbursement clears the organization's bank fraudulently through forgery or alteration. The term *embezzlement* applies to both billing and check-tampering schemes.

ACTION STEPS

▲ Identify the types of fraud that are most damaging to the organization.

▲ Assign responsibilities to segregate duties.

▲ Segregate authority for approving new vendors and purchasing.

Noncash Asset Misappropriation

Noncash misappropriation schemes are the third most costly form of asset-misappropriation schemes. These schemes can include the theft of physical assets and intellectual property.

The loss of valuable physical assets can cause a financial burden if such items need to be replaced. In addition, production delays and other inefficiencies may result if the stolen assets are critical to operations. Entity-wide procedures to secure physical assets are considered the best defense against this type of fraud. Management has the responsibility for creating these procedures, and audit committee members should examine the adequacy of controls over physical assets.

Theft of intellectual property poses its own challenges. While the company still retains its intellectual property after it is stolen, the use of stolen intellectual property by competitors can result in enormous setbacks in the marketplace. Intellectual property can include patents, trademarks, trade secrets, and copyrights. Intellectual property theft is sometimes overlooked as a form of fraud, perhaps because the loss to an organization can be invisible or take years to discover. The organization remains unaware of infringements until seizure and enforcement action is taken. Make no mistake: The losses related to stolen intellectual property can be significant. In 2010, the Justice Department issued a report on intellectual property enforcement and noted that there were 19,959 intellectual property seizures that year. The domestic value of the seized goods was $188.1 million. Had the seized goods been authentic, they would have had a retail value of $1.4 billion. The seizures resulted in 237 civil fines totaling $62,282,575.[17]

Most organizations have trade secrets, though they may not be inventoried or tracked like patents, trademarks, and copyrights. Trade secrets, as a subset of intellectual property, include chemical formulas, business plans, customer lists, and industrial processes. The exchange of trade secrets with third parties offers violators an unfair advantage in the marketplace. Organizations may find themselves particularly vulnerable to losing intellectual property upon an employee's departure. While nondisclosure and noncompete agreements can help thwart the loss of intellectual property, those determined to take advantage of someone's intellectual property will succeed. The leading Justice Department enforcement actions, termed "Significant Economic Espionage and Trade Secret Cases" in the 2010 *U.S. Intellectual Property Enforcement Coordinator Annual Report on Intellectual Property Enforcement*, involved the loss of trade secrets when an employee left an organization. Victim organizations included Dow, Goldman Sachs, Goodyear, Ford, Societe Generale, and Bristol-Myers Squibb.[18]

To protect organizational interests, precautions need to be taken to protect intellectual property. Passwords and restricted access are common protocols employed by organizations regardless of size or industry. The widespread use of thumb drives and peer-to-peer networks for working away from secure facilities should be examined in efforts to maintain control over intellectual property.

Aside from embezzlement and theft of intellectual property, the remaining asset-misappropriation schemes, such as falsified wages, false receipts, or false voids, while representing a drain on organizational resources, are unlikely to warrant board-level oversight, though line managers should, of course, continue to monitor and report such activity.

ACTION STEPS

▲ Utilize physical access controls, such as locks.

▲ Perform periodic asset inventories.

▲ Establish an intellectual property policy.

▲ Offer a whistle-blower hotline.

▲ Include a system feature to allow for remote swipe protocols on hardware.

▲ Maintain physical control over sensitive data.

▲ Encrypt files.

Financial Statement Fraud

Financial statement fraud involves the misstatement or omission of relevant financial statement data with the deliberate intention of misleading investors or creditors. Though accounting for less than 8 percent of fraud reported, it is by far the most costly type of fraud, with a median loss reported of $1 million, according to the ACFE 2012 *Report to the Nations on Occupational Fraud and Abuse* (see Figure 9.3).

Other organizations have collected data on the cost of financial statement fraud as well, and their numbers are even higher. COSO released a report on fraudulent financial reporting that analyzed fraud involving U.S. public companies reported between 1998 and 2007. There were 347 victim organizations examined with a cumulative misstatement of $120 billion. The mean loss was $400 million per case, and the median loss was $12.1 million. The sharp contrast between the mean and median loss suggests that just a few organizations suffered sizeable losses, pushing the mean higher than the median. Perhaps most alarming, COSO reported that stock values dropped 16.7 percent within two days of reported fraud.[19]

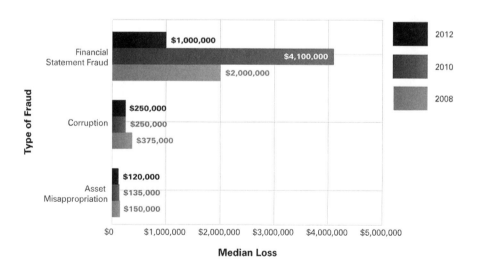

Figure 9.3   Median fraud loss by type.
Source: ACFE 2012 Report to the Nations on Occupational Fraud and Abuse

Of course, stock valuations can plunge even more than the average of 16.7 percent. Take the case of agricultural association Humboldt Creamery. It had a top valuation of $100 million but was sold at auction for $19.25 million in mid-2009 just months after fraud was discovered. In this case, the former CEO had deceived the auditors by inflating inventory amounts through the alleged use of stacked packaged milk powder to give the impression of higher quantities and by providing false financial information and supporting documents to secure an extension of an existing loan. According to COSO, the leading methods employed in financial statement fraud are revenue recognition, with a frequency of 61 percent, and overstated assets, with a frequency of 51 percent.[20] Typical revenue-recognition misstatements involved fictitious or premature sales, with frequent occurrences of premature sales. Sales may be considered unearned either because conditions to the sale have not yet been met or because sales are recorded for services not yet performed, as can occur with multiyear contracts.

Fraud related to overstated asset misstatements typically involves overvalued inventory and accounts receivable or inappropriately capitalized expenses. Another way to manipulate inventory valuation can arise when management aggressively allocates selling, general, and administrative expenses to the production process, with the result being overstated cost of goods sold and inventory for unsold units. Manipulating inventory overhead can be done either through the selection of the particular selling, including general and administrative expenses in the calculation, or by changing the percentage of the various selling, general, and administrative expenses allocated to manufacturing processes.

Waste Management, for example, used a variety of tricks in executing a financial statement fraud between 1992 and 1997, costing investors more than $6 billion through the inappropriate inflation of profits by $1.7 billion. Among other things, the SEC complaint alleged that senior executives at Waste Management "avoided depreciation expenses by both assigning unsupported and inflated salvage values and extending their useful lives, failed to record expenses for decreases in the value of landfills as they were filled with waste, refused to write off unsuccessful and abandoned landfill development projects, improperly capitalized expenses and maintained insufficient reserves for income taxes and other expenses."[21]

On the bright side, organizations can show great resiliency and recover from the ill effects of a fraud scheme. In just over a decade after suffering from fraud at the highest levels, Waste Management was named one of the World's Most Ethical Companies for 2009 and 2010 by the Ethisphere Institute. Per *Businessweek*'s 2002 listing of most improved boards, Waste Management made significant strides in improving its corporate governance position, including installing eight new members, all independent, on the nine-member board; naming a respected executive as audit committee chairman; banning side deals between directors and the company; and making changes to anti-shareholder governance policies, like staggered board elections, which are intended to promote management continuity at the expense of accountability to shareholders.[22]

The 2010 COSO report disclosed that 89 percent of the time when there was financial statement fraud, the CEO or the CFO was named as the offender.[23] Keep in mind that offenders need not have a direct financial gain from the distortions. Oftentimes, senior executives and owners engage in financial statement fraud to conceal subpar business performance, either to secure financing or meet investor expectations. They may be doing it to maintain their position and the prestige that comes with it.

Board and audit committee members have a role to play in both deterrence and detection of financial statement fraud. Deterrence efforts must focus on promoting an ethical work culture. In considering an organization's vulnerability to fraudulent financial statements, there are some specific areas on which to focus, specifically the domination of management by one person or a small group, significant related-party transactions, and highly complex transactions. On the detection front, analytical tools and third-party verification for management explanations of anomalies serve board members best in their efforts to detect financial statement fraud. (See Chapter 5 for more information on scrutinizing financial statements.)

ACTION STEPS

▲ Understand that financial statement fraud can lead to precipitous declines in stock prices and market value.

▲ Be mindful of fraud from all levels of the organization, as most fraud originates from the CEO or CFO.

▲ Actively review financial results, including ratio analytics, and challenge management explanations of unexpected results.

Fraud-Deterrence Tools

While fraud poses a tremendous threat to economic growth, there are several fraud-deterrence tools that organizations can utilize to reduce the cost of fraud. The ACFE has amassed enormous amounts of data on the effectiveness of various fraud-deterrence tools (see Figure 9.4). What's notable about the ranking of fraud-deterrence tools listed in Figure 9.4 is that the tools that top the list are the least expensive to administer.

This section outlines the most cost-effective fraud-deterrence tools that all organizations should implement, regardless of size. These include:

> Hotlines
> Employee support programs
> Surprise audits
> Ethics programs
  • Code of conduct and antifraud policy
  • Fraud training
> Mandatory vacations/job rotation
> Corporate culture

Median Loss Based on Presence of Antifraud Controls				
Control	Percent of Cases Implemented	Control in Place	Control Not in Place	Percent Reduction
Management Review	60.5%	$100,000	$185,000	45.9%
Employee Support Programs	57.5%	$100,000	$180,000	44.4%
Hotline	54.0%	$100,000	$180,000	44.4%
Fraud Training for Managers/Executives	47.4%	$100,000	$158,000	36.7%
External Audit of ICFR	67.5%	$120,000	$187,000	35.8%
Fraud Training for Employees	46.8%	$100,000	$155,000	35.5%
Antifraud Policy	46.6%	$100,000	$150,000	33.3%
Formal Fraud Risk Assessments	35.5%	$100,000	$150,000	33.3%
Internal Audit Fraud Examiner Department	68.4%	$120,000	$180,000	33.3%
Job Rotation/Mandatory Vacation	16.7%	$100,000	$150,000	33.3%
Surprise Audits	32.2%	$100,000	$150,000	33.3%
Rewards for Whistle-Blowers	9.4%	$100,000	$145,000	31.0%
Code of Conduct	78.0%	$120,000	$164,000	26.8%
Independent Audit Committee	59.8%	$125,000	$150,000	16.7%
Management Certification of Financial Statements	68.5%	$138,000	$164,000	15.9%
External Audit of Financial Statements	80.1%	$140,000	$145,000	3.4%

Figure 9.4   Median loss based on presence of antifraud controls.
Source: ACFE 2012 Report to the Nations on Occupational Fraud and Abuse

> ➤ Internal controls
>   - Segregation of duties
>   - Approvals and authorizations
>   - Account reconciliations
>   - Reports of financial performance
>   - Security of assets
>   - Information-system-controls policies and procedures
>   - Personnel policies, code of conduct, ethics policy, employee education, and enforcement
>   - Organizational structure, assignment of authority and responsibility, and employee selection processes

The listing of essential fraud-deterrence tools follows closely with the most effective fraud-deterrence tools reported by the ACFE. While data were not presented on the effectiveness of corporate culture and internal controls in reducing the cost and duration of fraud, corporate culture and internal controls serve as the foundation of governance upon which bookkeeping and financial reporting systems operate. As such, both corporate culture and internal controls must be included in board director and audit committee oversight efforts to reduce fraud. All these fraud-deterrence tools provide significant reductions in fraud losses and can be implemented in just a few days a year.

Hotlines

Anonymous tips are the leading source of initial detection of fraud schemes, with a detection rate of 43.3 percent (see Figure 9.5). Hotlines facilitate the process of providing anonymous tips by offering confidentiality to informants. While some informants may be willing to come forward without the presence of an anonymous whistle-blower

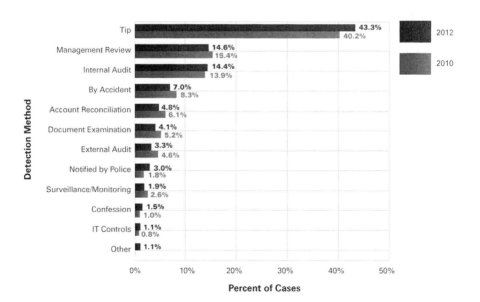

Figure 9.5   Fraud detection rate by detection method.
Source: ACFE 2012 Report to the Nations on Occupational Fraud and Abuse

hotline, data suggest that tips are more common when hotlines are available, and that 50.9 percent of these tips come through such hotlines.[24]

On the regulatory front, SOX requires audit committees to establish mechanisms for receiving complaints about irregularities in a company's accounting, auditing, and internal control systems. Note that this is not a requirement for a whistle-blower hotline; only a reporting mechanism must be provided. Listing contact names and phone numbers of company officers or directors in the code of conduct is considered sufficient notice of an organization's reporting mechanism. SOX also has provisions for stiff fines for retaliations against informants.

Aside from SOX, other whistle-blower protection laws and rules are in place to prevent retaliation against whistle-blowers, including the Whistleblower Protection Act of 1989, which protects government workers who report misconduct, and the Dodd-Frank Act, intended to strengthen the financial services industry by providing, among other things, assistance to whistle-blowers. Despite these protections, however, retaliation still occurs. And some whistle-blowers have found that they don't qualify for protection because they did not understand the legal provisions, which can be interpreted from case law. For example, in *Tides v. Boeing Co.*, the U.S. Ninth Circuit Court of Appeals excluded two Boeing auditors from SOX whistle-blower protection because the whistle-blowers went to the media instead of to approved recipients of information such as supervisors, law enforcement, or Congress.[25]

These two Boeing auditors were not the first to make the mistake of going first to the media. Robert McLean, a federal air marshal, did the same thing in 2003 when he expressed concern that air marshals would not be flying on long, nonstop flights in order to accommodate budget constraints within the Transportation Security Administration (TSA). He was fired soon after blowing the whistle, an act that prompted some to argue that he was the subject of retaliation.[26] McLean spent several years arguing his case. Even so, the limitation in his case that blocked him from receiving relief in the courts was that he blew the whistle through the media before exhausting options of reporting and resolving concerns internally with TSA.

In addition to the importance of using the right channels for anonymous tips, courts have also expressed their concern over informants making wild accusations. In 2006, a whistle-blower went to authorities with office gossip about possible fraudulent misstatements by Northwestern University in an effort to secure a more favorable bond rating and loans. When the claims proved baseless, the courts denied the informant whistle-blower protection, citing inadequate evidence.

These cases, while illustrating that care must be taken by prospective whistle-blowers to be sure their actions qualify for protection, may create such confusion as to what it takes to qualify for whistle-blower protection that potential informants may remain silent. Organizations that wish to mobilize their workforce to fight fraud should do their best to ensure that whistle-blowers feel comfortable coming forward by putting in place vigorous whistle-blower protection programs and clearly articulating the conditions to qualify for protection.

There are many highly qualified national providers of whistle-blower hotlines that give companies their own 800 number and handle complaints and tips, with 24/7/365 coverage. These companies have experienced operators who conduct a 15-to-20-minute intake interview and deliver an incident report to be distributed to key personnel within a client organization. A provision for anonymity to any individual who willingly comes forward to report a suspicion of fraud is critical to encouraging such reporting and should be a component of the organization's policy. Board directors and audit committee members must take great care to ensure that antiretaliation policies are in place and enforced.

Organizations that wish to engender trust with potential informants can do so by supporting a zero-tolerance policy for retaliation against whistle-blowers. Aside from a clear, strongly worded policy in support of whistle-blowers, protection for whistle-blowers can include expanded anonymous reporting systems with informant-identifier codes that allow informants to communicate with investigators. The

Ethics Resource Center reported in its 2009 National Business Ethics Survey that whistle-blower retaliations went down sharply in the presence of programs against whistle-blower retaliation, with retaliation occurring only 4 percent of the time, as opposed to 24 percent in organizations without a policy.[27]

Supporting whistle-blowers may go beyond simply prohibiting retaliation to involving rewards for informants, but a clear case cannot be made for offering rewards for whistle-blowers. Some chafe at the notion that personal enrichment would be involved in the motives of an informant. Data on the effectiveness of antifraud tools (see Figure 9.6) indicate that rewards for whistle-blowers reduce fraud by 59.1 percent. Conventional wisdom on rewards for whistle-blowers suggests that when rewards are offered, the amount of the

Duration of Fraud Based on Presence of Antifraud Controls				
Control	Percent of Cases Implemented	Control in Place	Control Not in Place	Percent Reduction
Job Rotation/Mandatory Vacation	16.7%	9 months	24 months	62.5%
Rewards for Whistle-Blowers	9.4%	9 months	22 months	59.1%
Surprise Audits	32.2%	10 months	24 months	58.3%
Code of Conduct	78.0%	14 months	30 months	53.3%
Antifraud Policy	46.6%	12 months	24 months	50.0%
External Audit of ICFR	67.5%	12 months	24 months	50.0%
Formal Fraud Risk Assessments	35.5%	12 months	24 months	50.0%
Fraud Training for Employees	46.8%	12 months	24 months	50.0%
Fraud Training for Managers/Executives	47.4%	12 months	24 months	50.0%
Hotline	54.0%	12 months	24 months	50.0%
Management Certification of Financial Statements	60.5%	12 months	24 months	50.0%
Independent Audit Committee	59.8%	13 months	24 months	45.8%
Internal Audit Fraud Examiner Department	68.4%	13 months	24 months	45.8%
Management Review	68.5%	14 months	24 months	41.7%
Employee Support Programs	57.5%	16 months	21 months	23.8%
External Audit of Financial Statements	80.1%	17 months	24 months	29.2%

Figure 9.6   Duration of fraud based on presence of antifraud controls.
Source: ACFE 2012 Report to the Nations on Occupational Fraud and Abuse

reward should be limited to a few thousand dollars. The criteria for awarding the rewards must be clear and measurable.

In rolling out a whistle-blower hotline, it is important to remember communication with trade partners. The ACFE 2012 *Report to the Nations on Occupational Fraud and Abuse* indicates that just 50.9 percent of tips come from employees, so it's imperative to extend the pool of available informants to include vendors and customers. Many companies include contact information for their whistle-blower hotline on the company's website, customer receipts, and vendor code-of-conduct agreements.

As a matter of procedure, the board of directors should approve protocols to ensure that reported fraud-related issues are dealt with appropriately. Ideally, the incident reports provided by the hotline should be examined by either the internal audit department or an external consultant (such as a certified fraud examiner or certified public accountant), who determines which complaints should be investigated further, referred to law enforcement, or dropped. Use of the internal audit department or outside consultant is crucial to giving potential whistle-blowers peace of mind in knowing that there will be no retribution for coming forward.

Employee Support Programs

Employee support programs offer psychiatric and credit counseling for employees. These programs have historically been viewed primarily as an employee benefit that improves morale by helping to support employees with problems that can otherwise sap productivity. Fraud survey data tell us that employee support programs have an added benefit of significantly reducing fraud losses. Data reported by the ACFE in 2012 indicate that the presence of employee support programs reduces fraud losses by 44 percent.

Employee support programs deliver outstanding results because they support employees with two of the critical elements fraudsters need to overcome: financial pressure and rationalization. Credit counseling can be very helpful in redirecting employees' efforts in more productive ways of fixing their problems than stealing. Perhaps more important, psychiatric counseling helps reduce rationalization for fraud, as root causes for problems and fresh solutions are discussed in counseling.

To better understand the mind of a fraud perpetrator, Dr. Donald Cressey, a sociologist and criminologist credited with many innovations in understanding criminal activity and specifically white-collar crime, developed the fraud triangle (see Figure 9.7) to explain how an otherwise trustworthy employee would steal. The three basic elements of the fraud triangle are rationalization, perceived opportunity, and financial pressure. The fraud triangle specifically excludes employees who seek out positions of trust in order to steal. According to the fraud triangle theory, an employee must be able to justify his or her actions (rationalization), find a way to both steal and conceal (perceived opportunity), and experience financial pressure in order to pursue a fraud scheme (financial pressure).

Rationalization peaks at the beginning of a fraud scheme. Anecdotal evidence supports this with accounts of fraud perpetrators who begin their fraud scheme with the intention of paying back their

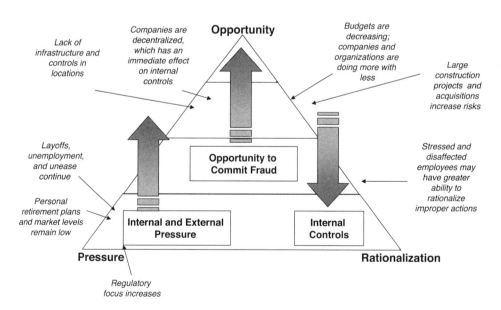

Figure 9.7   Fraud triangle.

ill-gotten gains, keeping a tally at the start, almost like an IOU. However, as the fraud scheme matures, many fraud perpetrators feel a decreased commitment to repay the money they've stolen, and they discontinue their tally of stolen money.

The importance of addressing rationalization at the beginning of a fraud scheme is further reinforced by data reported in the ACFE 2012 *Report to the Nations on Occupational Fraud and Abuse*. Figure 9.6, shown previously, shows that the duration of fraud schemes is reduced only marginally when employee support programs are in place, with employee support programs reducing the duration of fraud schemes by just five months, suggesting that perhaps employee support programs are of little benefit. However, the overwhelming benefit of employee support programs in a dollars sense does prove that employee support programs are effective in reducing the rationalization necessary to commit fraud. These divergent data points illustrate the importance of employees' using employee support programs before they start stealing because the need for rationalization is highest at the onset of a fraud scheme.

In a world where 80 percent of an organization's data is now unstructured, becoming aggressive and creative with text analytics is an effective and sufficient mechanism to prevent, detect, and monitor against fraud. Groundbreaking research released in 2009 jointly by the Association of Certified Fraud Examiners and Ernst & Young shows a correlation between certain key words related to the three elements of the fraud triangle and the onset of fraudulent activity. The study, led by Mike Sherrod and Vince Walden of Ernst & Young, considered the frequency of words appearing in emails associated with the three elements of the fraud triangle: opportunity, rationalization, and financial pressure.[28]

The effort to identify fraud schemes through email searches starts with the development of a set of key words that could suggest that fraudulent activity is occurring in an organization. Management needs to identify a separate set of key words for each of the three elements of the fraud triangle. The search words and phrases developed by Ernst & Young and the ACFE include:

> ➤ Rationalization: *I think it's okay, sounds reasonable, they owe me, I deserve, nobody will get hurt, won't miss it*

> ➤ Pressure: *make sales quota, under the gun, not comfortable, pull out all the stops, only a timing difference, spread*

> ➤ Opportunity: *override, special fees, off the books, side commission, back date, no receipt, smooth earnings, pull earnings forward*[29]

A deeper, richer list of key words is suggested, with organizations interested in testing unstructured data for the frequency of words associated with the three elements of the fraud triangle challenged to develop a data dictionary that includes internally relevant terms associated with fraudulent activities.

Once the key words are identified, data analytics can then search emails to identify not only the frequency of the various key words but also the employees frequently using these terms. The results of the search are twofold. First, a high frequency of key words for each of the three elements could suggest the likelihood of an ongoing fraud scheme. Second, the email search can identify the specific employees frequently using the key words, allowing investigators to focus their efforts on the key employees most likely to be involved in the fraud scheme.

As fraud schemes continue to reach new levels of sophistication, the ability to look at unstructured data such as emails is often one of the most effective ways to uncover elaborate schemes, especially those that involve corruption and collusion. Text analytics can be used to proactively and reactively monitor and detect for these hard-to-uncover fraud schemes. Although management is most responsible for this work, board directors and audit committee members can provide improved oversight of such fraud with an understanding of this issue.

Surprise Audits

Surprise audits are wonderfully effective fraud-deterrence tools because they do not need to be performed consistently or thoroughly to work. If the workforce is aware that surprise audits occur, the threat of detection serves as a strong deterrent. Unlike tedious tests of controls that may involve sample sizes for transactions of 50, 100, or even more, surprise audits can be effective with just a sample size of one. Board directors and audit committee members should endeavor to oversee management to be sure that they conduct surprise audits.

Ethics Programs

Research has provided ample proof that promoting an ethical work environment not only saves money but makes money. The Ethisphere Institute released its 2011 list of the World's Most Ethical Companies supported by financial performance data that show those companies outperformed the S&P 500 index before, during, and after the 2008 recession, with returns beating the S&P index by 25 percentage points in 2009 and 35 percentage points in 2010 and early 2011.[30] (See Figure 9.8.)

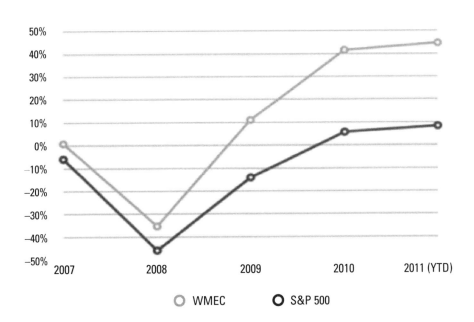

Figure 9.8   Percent returns, World's Most Ethical Companies versus S&P 500.
Source: Ethisphere Institute

Ethics programs vary greatly among various organizations. While an ethics program can be scaled to the size of the organization, even the smallest organizations can reap the fraud-deterrent benefits offered by having a code of conduct, antifraud policy, and fraud training. The ACFE 2012 *Report to the Nations on Occupational Fraud and Abuse* indicates that each of those three elements of an ethics program offers significant reductions in median fraud losses (see Figure 9.7 on page 170). Since these tools can be effectively implemented in just a few days a year, every organization should use its ethics program as a key fraud-deterrent strategy.

Publicly traded companies may already have robust ethics programs in place as a way of satisfying regulatory requirements under SOX, though there is a big difference between having a compliance program on paper and having one that is truly embraced and meets the spirit of the law. In addition, even privately held companies can find that having an effective ethics program is advantageous if they face litigation subject to Federal Sentencing Guidelines, because the guidelines specify seven elements of an effective compliance program necessary in order to qualify for lighter sentencing. Common types of white-collar crime subject to guidelines include embezzlement, mail fraud, wire fraud, Internet fraud, bank fraud, money laundering, mortgage fraud, real estate fraud, securities violations, government contract fraud, and tax fraud (see Chapter 7 for more information about Federal Sentencing Guidelines).

Given the exposure that public and private organizations face with regard to the effectiveness of their ethics program, board and audit committee members should monitor their program as a key oversight function.

Code of Conduct and Antifraud Policy

Ethics policies serve an essential function in taking away the "stupidity defense" often employed by fraud perpetrators because, without a written standard of behavior, violators can excuse their behavior by saying they didn't know any better.

Ethics policies and codes of conduct serve distinct purposes, though they may be presented in the same document. Codes of conduct present a more top-level view, general outline of an organization's policies that include an ethics policy as well as other company policies. An ethics policy is more detailed in stating expectations of behavior and should specifically address risks of employee misconduct specific to the organization's industry and manner of operation. For example, cash-based businesses should enumerate appropriate ways to handle and use cash. Organizations that frequently expect their personnel to travel should include specific travel and entertainment policies in the ethics policy. (Chapter 8 on risk management discusses how risks specific to an organization can be identified.)

There is no shortage of suggested ethics policies. At a minimum, an organization's ethics policy should:

➤ Address the company's right to inspect desks, lockers, and electronic data held on hard drives, thumb drives, and smartphones. If video surveillance or credit monitoring is used, that should be mentioned in the policy as well.

➤ Include a definition of proprietary information, which may include customer lists, trade secrets, and even suppliers.

➤ Include a document-retention policy to protect the organization from possible obstruction-of-justice charges by ensuring employees are aware that discoverable evidence should not be destroyed when litigation is pending.

➤ Include a gift policy that specifies what gifts employees are allowed to receive in the course of executing their duties. Some organizations choose to have a low dollar limit for gifts or even prohibit all gifts in an effort to reduce the persuasive influence of gifts received.

➤ Include a statement on what relationships may give rise to a conflict of interest, with a provision requiring self-disclosure of any related-party transactions.

➤ List punishments for violations.

Fraud Training

Fraud training reduced median losses by one-half, making fraud training for employees and managers one of the ACFE's top five most effective fraud-deterrence tools (see Figure 9.6 on page 168). Unfortunately, ACFE data suggest that fraud training was performed at only 47 percent of victim organizations. Board and audit committee members can do their part to improve participation in training initiatives by tying satisfactory completion of fraud training to incentives and rewards deemed important to personnel, such as bonuses, paycheck distribution, or attendance at desirable company events. Senior level management participation in training events sends a strong message of support. For their part, board and audit committee members can also attend fraud training events to reinforce the importance of training.

Another critical area for board oversight of training is ensuring that trade partners receive fraud training specific to the contracts entered into by both parties. Specifically, regulators have extended accountability for anticorruption programs to vendors, affiliates, and agents. It may be more difficult to command full attendance to fraud training by third parties, in which case it may be necessary to request placement of fraud training in the agenda of an existing employee meeting within affiliate organizations that are expected to have high attendance.

Mandatory Vacations/Job Rotation

Some fraud schemes require continuous presence to avoid detection. Imagine the clerk who must be present for bank reconciliations. That clerk will not want to take vacation at the time of the month bank statements arrive. Mandatory vacation encourages job rotation as coworkers learn key duties performed within their team, improving team readiness for layoffs or other personnel changes. Although setting vacations and job rotations falls under the purview of management, board directors and audit committee members should understand the importance of these tools in detecting and preventing fraud.

Corporate Culture

"Tone at the top" is often correlated with corporate culture. It refers to the importance of ethical leadership in forming a strong antifraud work culture. Employees watch management closely and use the conduct of senior management and board members as a benchmark for acceptable behavior. If employees observe senior managers acting in a self-serving manner, they are more likely to tolerate unethical behavior in themselves and their coworkers. Alternately, leadership by senior executives and board members that is based on integrity and honesty builds loyalty and trust.

Unfortunately, employees are too often exposed to maladaptive behavior that reduces organizational loyalty. The Ethics Resource Center reported in its 2005 National Business Ethics Survey that employees commonly observed the following types of misconduct that injure organizational pride and loyalty:

> ➤ Abusive or intimidating behavior toward employees
> ➤ Lying to employees, customers, vendors, or the public
> ➤ Situations that place employee interests over organizational interests
> ➤ Violations of safety regulations
> ➤ Misreporting of actual time worked
> ➤ Discrimination on the basis of race, color, gender, age, or similar categories
> ➤ Stealing or theft
> ➤ Sexual harassment[31]

Effective implementation of antifraud tools is impossible without a strong antifraud culture to support it. Several factors contribute to good "tone at the top," including setting reasonable performance goals, tempering efforts to meet analyst expectations, careful observation of performance-based compensation, and consistent disciplining of ethical violations. Board directors, audit committee members, and management should work together to set an appropriate tone that filters down through all levels of the organization.

Internal Controls

Internal controls are those processes instituted to ensure that information is accurately recorded and reported. Set by management and overseen by the board, properly designed and implemented internal controls improve operational efficiency and regulatory compliance and reduce fraud losses. Poorly designed internal controls lead to distorted information that exposes companies to inadequate management decision making, violations of laws and regulations, and ignorance about fraud losses incurred.

Internal control principles are universal. However, implementation varies widely based on the resources and support senior management provides. Low levels of controls provide ample opportunity for occupational fraud. Yet care must be taken in determining the right amount of internal controls to implement. Employing high levels of internal controls can be as damaging to an organization as low levels of controls, because organizations that utilize too many controls may find that resources allocated to internal controls starve other organizational priorities as well as hamper operational efficiency.

Since there is not a "correct" amount of controls, management, board directors, and audit committee members must work together to evaluate the adequacy of internal controls by examining the ability of existing controls to address key organizational vulnerabilities. Certain vulnerabilities are common to most organizations, while other vulnerabilities surface through the risk-assessment process.

The fundamental general controls applicable to most organizations are:

> Segregation of duties
> Approvals and authorizations
> Account reconciliations
> Reports of financial performance

> Security of assets

> Information-system-controls policies and procedures

> Personnel policies, code of conduct, ethics policy, employee education, and enforcement

> Organizational structure, assignment of authority and responsibility, and employee selection processes

Segregation of Duties

Embezzlement represents one of the more embarrassing frauds board directors face because the most expensive embezzlements are due to an overreliance on the trustworthiness of one of an organization's top executives. Segregation of duties aims to deter fraud by eliminating the ability of any one individual to complete enough steps in a transaction to both steal and conceal. With properly designed segregation of duties, employees can still steal, but they would have to enlist the help of a coworker, increasing the possibility of detection. Conspiracies are hard to maintain over the long term, making segregation of duties an appealing fraud-deterrence tool.

Generally speaking, segregating duties seeks to separate the recording, authorization, and custody of any transaction cycle. Stated more specifically, the University of California Office of the President states in its *Understanding Internal Controls* report that "no one person should initiate the transaction, approve the transaction, record the transaction, reconcile balances, handle assets, or review reports."[32]

Some organizations go light on both segregation of duties and internal controls, mostly because of the small scale of the organization. Smaller organizations may assert that adequate segregation of duties is out of reach because of limited resources. However, organization size is no excuse for not having adequate segregation of duties.

Larger organizations typically have well designed and tested internal controls that prevent the same employee from being able to perform a combination of transactions that can divert funds without detection. Large organizations are more likely to experience a blind spot in applying internal controls and segregation of duties conventions when it comes to high-level executives, depositing too much trust to a single key person as the leader.

The division of tasks for two-, three-, and four-person offices shown in Figures 9.9, 9.10, and 9.11 comes from the Vermont State Auditor and satisfies the goal of segregated duties.[33]

Organizations should be particularly careful to ensure that duties segregated by design are enforced by the accounting software instead of just by company policy and convention. Although management is largely responsible for this task, it behooves board directors and audit committee members to understand this issue so they can improve oversight.

Even with computer-enforced segregations of duties, such as user-name and password protocols for various types of transactions, organizations must be on the lookout for dominant senior executives who can enroll a subordinate either knowingly or unknowingly into playing a part in an embezzlement scheme that the senior manager alone cannot play.

Such was the case with the Koss Corp. fraud that was detected in 2009 that cost shareholders over $30 million. In its filing against

Accountant or Other
Financial Personnel

> Record pledges
> Mail checks
> Write checks
> Reconcile bank statements
> Record credits/debits
> Approve payroll
> Disburse petty cash
> Authorize purchase orders
> Authorize check requests
> Authorize invoices for payment

A receptionist or administrative employee could open mail and create a deposit log

Executive Director

> Receive and open bank statements
> Sign checks
> Make deposits
> Perform interbank transfers
> Distribute paychecks
> Review petty cash
> Review bank reconciliations
> Approve vendor invoices
> Perform analytical procedures
> Sign important contracts
> Make compensation adjustments
> Discuss matters with board of directors or audit committee

In addition, nonaccounting personnel such as a receptionist or program personnel can be trained to perform some of the less technical duties. Board members can be used to further segregate duties.

Figure 9.9   Segregation of duties, two-person office.

Accounting Staff

- Record pledges
- Write checks
- Reconcile bank statements
- Record credits/debits
- Reconcile petty cash
- Distribute payroll

Executive Director

- Sign important contracts
- Make compensation adjustments
- Discuss matters with board of directors or audit committee
- Sign checks
- Complete deposit slips
- Perform interbank transfers
- Perform analytical procedures
- Review bank reconciliations

Accountant or Other
Financial Personnel

- Approve payroll
- Process vendor invoices
- Mail checks
- Perform analytical procedures
- Aprove invoices for payment
- Disburse petty cash
- Open mail and log cash
- Receive bank statements

In addition, nonaccounting personnel such as a receptionist or program personnel can be trained to perform some of the less technical duties. Board members can be used to further segregate duties.

Figure 9.10   Segregation of duties, three-person office.

Accounting Staff

- Record pledges
- Write checks
- Reconcile bank statements
- Record credits/debits
- Reconcile petty cash

Executive Director

- Sign important contracts
- Make compensation adjustments
- Discuss matters with board of directors or audit committee
- Sign checks
- Perform analytical procedures

Accountant/Other

- Distribute payroll
- Open mail and log cash
- Disburse petty cash
- Mail checks
- Receive bank reconciliations

Accountant/Other

- Approve vendor invoices
- Perform interbank transfers
- Approve payroll
- Complete deposit slips

In addition, nonaccounting personnel such as a receptionist or program personnel can be trained to perform some of the less technical duties. Board members can be used to further segregate duties.

Figure 9.11   Segregation of duties, four-person office.

two of Koss's accounting personnel, the SEC alleged that "since at least 2004, [Sujata] Sachdeva—the former Principal Accounting Officer, Secretary and Vice-President of Finance at Koss—stole over $30 million from Koss. Sachdeva used the embezzled funds to finance an extravagant lifestyle, including lavish spending sprees at department stores, designer boutiques, jewelry stores, and other high-end retailers. . . . Sachdeva and senior accountant [Julie] Mulvaney attempted to hide the embezzlement on Koss's balance sheet and income statement by overstating assets, expenses, and cost of sales, and by understating liabilities and sales."[34]

As noted in the SEC filing, Sachdeva enjoyed great trust within the organization, holding three positions simultaneously. The multitasking didn't end there. Michael Koss, an anthropology major, held the position of Sachdeva's direct report as chief financial officer and four other titles as well: vice chairman, chief executive officer, chief operating officer, and president.[35] All other things being equal, having a nonfinance person hold the CFO position is a huge red flag, not to mention the difficulty in anyone's effectively executing Koss's various duties that the five titles implied. Though the Koss fraud may be an extreme example of lax governance practices, it does illustrate the importance of guarding against unfettered control by senior executives.

Approvals and Authorizations

Care and effort must be taken in deciding who has the ability to approve transactions. Although management is largely responsible for making this decision, board directors and audit committee members should be aware of the issue, monitor approval rights, and ask questions when red flags are raised.

For example, transactions related to multiyear contracts such as leases or purchase orders can be of particular concern because the effects of a bad agreement could haunt an organization for years. Organizations should be just as careful in deciding who can authorize long-term purchase contracts, since the execution of such agreements often requires cash or loans.

Title inflation can occur when organizations are overly generous with increased titles in lieu of increased salaries. The danger organizations run with such title inflation is that official-sounding titles like "vice president" might give the impression to counterparties in the business community that a certain level of authority is implied in the title.

Account Reconciliations

Account reconciliations, which involve the comparison of data between two sets of records, such as a receiving log and a payable report, serve a critical function in deterring and detecting fraud. Account reconciliations can be used to, among other things, ensure amounts paid or received are correct, goods/services have been received, and appropriate authorization occurred. Management, board directors, and audit committee members should work together to ensure that reconciliations are routinely performed and that personnel involved with processing steps to the transaction are not involved with completing them.

Reports of Financial Performance

Reports of financial performance against budgets, forecasts, competitors, and history can serve as an early warning sign of either business waste or occupational fraud. The design of internal reports that evaluate performance should be approached with economy and purpose. There are countless metrics and ratios, also known as key performance indicators, that can be included in financial performance reports. The skill comes in deciding which few to include. It is a decision typically made by management with oversight from the board. Some consider seven or eight to be an ideal dashboard. Selection of the key performance indicators should contemplate risks identified in the risk-assessment process that are specific to the organization.

The need for economy in the selection comes from the need to focus attention on actionable data. All too often, internal reports and board packets have so much data that it can be difficult to see growing problems. Sometimes, reports get bloated because items included once in a report are repeated in subsequent reports without thought as to the current need. Other times, copious data may be included as a way for top management to provide data for the sake of relieving its conscience about sensitive issues. Some staffers may feel that including data in a report may fulfill their responsibility in delicate matters. Information drives agenda. Care should be taken in what board members look at when reviewing financial performance.

Security of Assets

Secure facilities serve as a general control by safeguarding assets from occupational and third-party theft. Noncash misappropriation schemes, which include employees stealing inventory or equipment, are the third most costly form of asset-misappropriation schemes. Therefore, organizations should make sure that high-value items are identified and secured. In addition, providing perimeter security and updating codes and keys periodically also improve security of assets. These are tasks undertaken by management and overseen by board directors and audit committee members.

Information-System-Controls Policies and Procedures

Information-system-controls policies and procedures should be set at the entity-level to ensure that electronic data access and privileges reinforce company standards for confidentiality as well as support efforts to segregate duties through user-name and password protocols.

Personnel Policies, Code of Conduct, Ethics Policy, Employee Education, and Enforcement

The creation of organizational policies and employee training assist organizational goals by stating expected behavior so that ignorance cannot be a defense and violations can be enforced. However, remember that the written word works best when it is reinforced by strong tone at the top, as evidenced by honorable actions by top management.

Organizational Structure, Assignment of Authority and Responsibility, and Employee Selection Processes

The design of the organization chart dictates lines of authority and reporting lines, which are crucial in defining decision rights and information flow, resulting in either opaque or transparent governance. Aside from governance issues, choice in assignment of authority and responsibility can affect morale and efficiency. Overly restrictive authorization protocols hamper efficiency and lead to waste and ineffective allocations of resources. Furthermore, it can frustrate employees and lower morale when employees are given responsibility for an area but not the attendant authority. Periodic consideration of the organizational structure and the assignment of authority and responsibility ensure that organizational strategies can be carried out effectively and efficiently.

Hiring protocols also serve as a general control. Suggested employment screening tools such as background checks, employment and education verification, and credit checks are essential steps to ensuring that new hires can effectively perform their assigned responsibilities as well as possibly sparing the organization from hiring someone likely to steal.

ACTION STEPS

▲ Use text analytics to monitor and detect fraud schemes.

▲ Identify key performance indicators that should be included in financial performance reports in order to help identify risks specific to the organization.

▲ Undertake periodic review of the organizational structure and the assignment of authority and responsibility in order to ensure that organizational strategies are carried out effectively and efficiently.

▲ Be sure to encrypt all sensitive or even potentially sensitive files.

CHAPTER TEN

Expect the Unexpected

FEW THINGS are worse than getting caught unaware, especially when it's bad news. To protect shareholder value, boards must anticipate not just bad outcomes through active risk management but also crisis response so that bad news is addressed swiftly. In this chapter, we outline crisis-management and crisis-media plans, board-level fraud responses, and succession planning principles to ensure continuity in two key management roles that affect the audit committee: the chief financial officer and the chief audit executive.

The Need for Crisis-Management and Crisis-Media Plans

Headline news related to ethical scandals derailed the succession plans of two well-respected business titans, Warren Buffett and Rupert Murdoch, in 2011. In the case of Buffett, the corporate scandal involved the use of insider information by his heir apparent at Berkshire Hathaway, David Sokol. Buffett had specifically prohibited the practice of inner-circle management proposing investments in which a senior staffer had an existing or imminent financial interest. But Sokol just couldn't help himself. He went ahead and bought a stake in Lubrizol, a manufacturer of specialty chemicals, just before Berkshire

Hathaway took a $9 billion stake in the company. According to statements from Warren Buffett and Lubrizol regulatory filings, Sokol purchased Lubrizol prior to suggesting the potential takeover of Lubrizol by Berkshire Hathaway.[1] Sokol later resigned amid the ensuing controversy. Buffett also took a share of the blame in the public eye when he was less than forthcoming in initial press dealings as to the reasons for Sokol's unexpected departure.[2]

Rupert Murdoch also faced succession concerns but closer to home, because the heir apparent of his giant media business was his son. James Murdoch, deputy chief operating officer of News Corp., saw his career implode shortly after his testimony in front of British Parliament in 2011 was disputed by two high-level News Corp. executives. The scandal that reached the C-suite started in the newsroom at the UK tabloid *News of the World*, where phone hacking to intercept voice-mail messages allegedly occurred. While public sentiment seemed more tolerant of tabloid journalism when the hacking involved celebrities, politicians, and the royal family, the News Corp. scandal cut deeper. Public sentiment turned against the company when it was revealed that the phone intercepts involved conversations regarding the disappearance of a 13-year-old. This headline-grabbing scandal became a cautionary tale in corporate governance when James Murdoch's judgment was called into question. The complaints took two tacks: the limited scope of the investigations ordered by senior leadership at News Corp. and the appearance of tolerance by senior leadership for unethical behavior on the part of journalists.

Many considered the scope of the investigations to be insufficient considering the nature of the allegations. News Corp. underwrote only two investigations. The first, in 2006, was a preliminary investigation in the wake of the arrest of Glenn Mulcaire and *News of the World* royal editor Clive Goodman. The second investigation, in 2007, supposedly was more expansive. The second investigation was considered inadequate because the questions prescribed in the investigation of five editors related to Goodman.[3] The results of the investigations led senior executives to conclude that the ethical breaches were limited in nature. Such limited investigations do not communicate a zealous search for truth.

James Murdoch's judgment was called into question when witnesses came forth indicating that he knew as early as 2008 that ethical breaches extended beyond just one reporter, suggesting that not only did Murdoch perjure himself before Parliament when he denied any knowledge of widespread practices of hacking, but also that he was tolerant of widespread ethical breaches because he knew of the breaches and did not take corrective action. Murdoch's behavior runs counter to best practices in corporate governance that promote zero tolerance of unethical behavior and set a strong ethical tone at the top with leadership by example.[4]

Headline-making accounting scandals in the United States have also shaken the trust of mainstream America, which all too often seems to believe that the powers that be are looking out for them and that Wall Street makes good use of the resources contributed to economic development in the form of shareholder investment. Scandals like Enron and Lehman Brothers present a very different picture of corporate governance, illustrating a gross lack of ethical leadership that ended up with deferred retirements and lost homes.

As we have seen, it is not unusual for stock prices to drop surrounding an earnings restatement, highlighting the need for the audit committee to manage the aftermath of bad news in efforts to effectively steward shareholder resources. With little margin for error in the first few days after the announcement of bad financial news, audit committees and board directors must be sure that organizations have crisis-management and crisis-media plans in place, and they must designate members of the crisis-management team and crisis-media team before the unthinkable happens. Members of the crisis-management and crisis-media teams are selected by management and may not necessarily include the same individuals.

Although they may not be directly involved in crisis management, board directors need to be prepared for the unexpected, especially for potentially catastrophic scenarios that can quickly destroy shareholder value. This includes having an emergency succession plan for the CEO, and possibly CFO, in the event quick action is needed to address a governance crisis.

Members of the Crisis-Management Team

The crisis-management team helps to mitigate any ill effects of the crisis. Crisis-management team members, selected by management, should be impaneled in advance. The team may include representatives from the public relations, legal, security, operations, finance, and human resources departments. It is important to have 24-hour contact information for all crisis-management members. When impaneling a crisis-management team, the organization also needs to designate a team leader and a spokesperson, which need not be a shared role.

Important elements of any crisis-management plan should include steps to minimize losses, initiate the crisis-media plan, and notify the proper authorities as deemed necessary, which may include regulators and external auditors.

Members of the Crisis-Media Team

The crisis-media team serves as the first line of defense during a negative event, operating under the leadership of the organization's official spokesperson. Aside from the spokesperson, additional crisis-media-team members may be added depending on the resources available, size of organization, and severity of the crisis. Organizations may want to outsource the role of spokesperson to skilled public relations firms, hiring a professional crisis communicator, a move that often proves prudent when making controversial announcements when bad news hits.

At the onset of a crisis, management should direct its staff to take efforts to scrub the organization's website and other online outlets of any content that may be deemed inappropriate in light of current events. Next, the crisis-media team should develop a set of talking points that can be clearly and consistently communicated. Depending on the scope of the crisis, it may be prudent to develop separate messaging for internal and external audiences. Although, as mentioned, board directors and audit committee members may not be directly involved in these efforts, they all should be aware of related goings-on and they should understand management's motives undertaken to solve the crisis and blunt any related scandal.

While there can be many sources for scandals, the issues that audit committees are likely to encounter in terms of media management relate to accounting errors attributed to ethical breaches, so communications should first assert the organization's commitment to restoring trust. Many questions posed to victim organizations can be anticipated. At a minimum, the crisis-media team should have answers prepared for the following questions:

> When was the matter discovered?

> Has this happened before? If so, when?

> What is the organization's policy on this matter?

> What affect will this matter have on shareholders? Creditors? Vendors? Customers?

> Who discovered the issue?

> How long has the issue been occurring without notice?

> What is being done to recover losses?

> Will there be an investigation?

> Who will head the investigation?

> Has anything been done to mitigate the risk of recurrence?

ACTION STEPS

▲ Set up crisis-management and crisis-media teams in advance.

▲ Have 24-hour contact information for all crisis-management members.

▲ Anticipate stakeholder concerns in crisis-media communications.

Board-Level Fraud Response

With fraud losses estimated at 5 percent of GDP, it is rare that an organization can escape the reach of fraud. Lack of adequate investigation of suspected fraud has been the source of deep regret for directors of various organizations, including infoGroup Inc. and DHB Industries.

InfoGroup audit committee chairman Vasant Raval was prosecuted for inadequately investigating fraud. In response to allegations of self-dealing by the CEO, Raval conducted a one-man investigation in 2005 that lasted 12 days. According to reports, the audit committee chairman's investigation did not include investigating the CEO's expenses.[5]

At DHB Industries, the SEC charged three outside directors, Gary Nadelman, Jerome Krantz, and Cary Chasin, who all served on the company's audit committee, with being "willfully blind to numerous red flags" of "massive accounting fraud." The SEC charged that DHB was engaged in pervasive fraud, misappropriated company assets, and filed false and misleading reports to investors.[6]

The SEC's response to the inadequate investigation on the part of these board directors was severe. In the case of infoGroup, the audit committee chairman was fined $100,000 and barred from serving as an officer or director for five years. In the case of DHB, each ex-director was fined, with penalties of $820,000 for Nadelman, $375,000 for Krantz, and $100,000 for Chasin. All three have been barred for life from serving as officers or directors of a public company.[7]

The SEC has said that it does not wish to concern itself with the majority of hard-working board directors. "We will not second-guess the good-faith efforts of directors. But in stark contrast, Krantz, Chasin and Nadelman were directors and audit committee members who repeatedly turned a blind eye to warning signs of fraud and other misconduct by company officers," said Robert Khuzami, director of the SEC's Division of Enforcement.[8]

One of the key lessons to be learned from such scandals is that board directors and audit committee members must be vigilant in their investigations into allegations of fraud. They must devote adequate resources to address fraud. The SEC has ramped up enforcement efforts, having brought cases covering a broad spectrum of financial wrongdoing in 2011 totaling $2.8 billion in penalties and disgorgement,[9] a substantial increase from the penalties charged in 2008, of $1.03 billion.[10]

To avoid the pitfalls suffered by the boards at infoGroup and DHB Industries, audit committees and board directors should be aware of typical fraud allegations requiring board-level response, key fraud-investigation principles, and steps in the fraud-response-plan.

Fraud Allegations Requiring Board-Level Response

To address fraud, many organizations have protocols in place to investigate and punish fraudulent actions. Because of the pervasive nature of fraud, it is unreasonable to involve the board of directors in every fraud incident, as most fraud is addressed satisfactorily by management. Management involved in the fraud-response team can include the legal, human resources, internal audit, operations, and investigations (if such a unit exists apart from internal audit) departments. Those in management charged with fraud response should have clear guidelines for which fraud cases to bring to the attention of the board. Fraud allegations that should require prompt board involvement include:

> **Financial Reporting and Disclosure Obligations and Accounting Improprieties:** These types of violations may include departures from GAAP, such as revenue recognition or unreported liabilities that would affect investor decisions or loan covenants.

> **Diversions of Company Funds and/or Inappropriate Purchases:** These types of fraud typically involve inappropriate related-party transactions or senior executives who inappropriately classify personal expenditures as corporate expenses.

> **Negligent Contract Administration:** Board-level response may be necessary when allegations surface about negligent contract

administration, especially government contracts for which breach-of-contract claims make the dollar value of the violations irrelevant.

> **Inadequate Internal Controls:** This is specifically a concern for board members of publicly traded organizations that report on internal controls over financial reporting (ICFR) because of the civil and criminal penalties that attach to unreported inadequacies in internal controls.

> **Suspicious Market Trading:** Insider trading can be prosecuted regardless of reported gains, making a dollar-value assessment a poor guideline for management in deciding when to include board members in fraud response.

> **High-Dollar Frauds:** What constitutes a high-dollar fraud varies by organization and can depend greatly depending on the capital at risk, operating returns, cash flows, and other shareholder concerns.

> **Frauds Involving Senior Management:** Who is considered senior management varies by organization size and structure and may include, but not necessarily be limited to, roles with the words *president, vice president,* or *chief* in their title. In frauds involving senior management, dollar values are irrelevant. Board involvement and the use of outside resources to investigate are recommended.

Key Fraud-Investigation Principles

When it comes to high-level fraud investigations that involve board-level leadership, board members must focus on four principles to avert criticism for their involvement in the resolution of any high-profile fraud: consistency, skepticism, authenticity, and credibility.

> **Consistency:** Consistency in the completion of any fraud investigation is essential. Determining a core set of investigation steps that are followed in each and every fraud investigation defends the organization against accusations of surreptitious prosecution. If investigation steps are cut or the investigation is terminated, the reason why

must be documented. This applies to all fraud investigations, but especially to high-profile fraud allegations.

> **Skepticism:** Skepticism in apprehending the facts of the case is a key principle in fraud investigations. Beyond mere doubt, skepticism encompasses a mindful approach that considers all things are possible and requires investigators to consider all of the possible methods for deceit, regardless of the likelihood. Skepticism of high-profile suspects may be difficult for board members who may have developed bonds based on common experiences or similar backgrounds. In such cases, it is suggested that the board refer the fraud investigation to external fraud investigators to avoid the appearance of influence. In addition, board members should keep an open mind as to how widespread a fraud may reach within the C-suite before narrowing in on just one target for an investigation.

> **Authenticity:** To be believable, fraud investigations must be genuine and thorough. The two high-profile fraud cases mentioned earlier in this chapter involving James Murdoch of News Corp. and Vasant Raval of infoGroup Inc. demonstrated very limited fraud investigations. In the case of News Corp., having investigators examine just 300 emails related to five specific reporters tied to the disgraced reporter would not be sufficient to eliminate the concern that phone tapping extended beyond just one rogue reporter. Similarly, a 12-day investigation performed by just one person, as was the case with Raval of infoGroup, is unlikely to prove sufficient effort was expended in the investigation. To avoid the appearance of an inauthentic investigation, boards should have a set protocol for investigations that will more than likely extend beyond just one investigator, except perhaps in those cases in which that one individual is a trained fraud investigator. Better to cast a wide net early and narrow it once the facts warrant limitations to the investigation.

> **Credibility:** The resolution of a high-profile fraud investigation, whether it results in no action or in the termination or legal prosecution of the suspect, must stand up to the scrutiny of a far-reaching web of regulators, law-enforcement officials, insurers, shareholders, and

the media. In addition, a mishandled fraud investigation can jeopardize successful prosecution. The selection of the investigation team sets the tone for the investigation and is essential to squashing any doubts on the soundness of the investigation's outcome. Board members should focus on the qualifications of the team members, adequacy of skill sets prescribed (e.g., computer forensics, investigations, fraud examinations), and the resources made available for the investigation.

Steps in the Fraud-Response Plan

Ideally, a fraud investigation accomplishes three goals: investigate fraud allegations, punish known violations, and remediate processes that allowed the fraud to occur. Throughout an investigation and in response to it, boards must ensure fair treatment of employees and uphold employee rights, as well as mitigate losses with respect to physical assets, stock prices, and reputation.

While many investigations do not require board involvement, the board should take an active role in developing the organization's standard fraud-investigation protocol. Investigation methodologies, such as collecting and analyzing evidence and report writing, are well-developed areas of study that do not require specific direction by the board, with decisions on standard operating procedures best left to those performing the investigations, typically an investigations unit or internal auditors. However, board directors should have a say in the design of the investigation protocol in the areas of receiving and evaluating complaints, preserving evidence and assets, assembling the investigation team, responding to findings, and concluding the investigation.

Receive and Evaluate Complaints

As we have seen, anonymous tips are the leading source of initial detection, with 43.3 percent of frauds identified through tips, according the ACFE 2012 *Report to the Nations on Occupational Fraud and Abuse*, far outperforming management review, which discovers fraud about 15 percent of the time, and internal audit, which has a detection rate of about 14 percent. The importance of tips cannot be stressed enough. Tips may come from a variety of sources, with more than 50 percent of tips coming from outside the company. Audit committees, and boards that lack an audit committee and therefore collectively fulfill the audit committee function, should have a process in place for receiving tips.

As mentioned, setting up a protocol for processing tips provided to the whistle-blower hotline or other reporting mechanism is a responsibility of the audit committee. Reporting lines for individuals that are included in the distribution list of reported tips typically include a member of the audit committee.

Such a system for receiving tips should include a process of identifying which tips require further investigation or perhaps referral to a different department. Tips should be evaluated for merit as well as significance, with high-dollar and high-profile tips sent immediately to the audit committee. Consideration should be given to alerting insurers, regulators, and external auditors for certain types of fraud allegations.

While some organizations would prefer to postpone disclosure until the magnitude of restatement is known, publicly traded companies may be required to make a public filing within days or, at most, weeks. Additional public findings that would require disclosure of the existence of the investigation without knowing the severity include periodic SEC filings, earnings releases, or initial public offerings.

As a practical matter, some organizations are hesitant to include external auditors early in an investigation because, upon notice of a fraud allegation, the external auditor is likely to recommend its own investigation—with all the fees that go along with it. A cost-benefit analysis should be considered at this point because, while it may be appealing to put off incurring what may end up being unnecessary auditor fees, if something reportable does emerge, the auditor will likely duplicate internal investigations as part of its due diligence, and total investigation costs may be twice what they would have been had the external auditors been involved with the investigation from the beginning.

Preserve Evidence and Assets

Immediate efforts to preserve evidence and protect assets should be taken at the beginning of a fraud investigation. Although this responsibility generally falls to management, board directors and audit committee members should be aware of any and all steps undertaken during a fraud investigation.

One of the most common first steps undertaken in fraud examinations is to place suspects on administrative leave and secure their work stations. Consideration should be given to existence of possible co-conspirators who may remain behind after the removal of the suspected perpetrator. Boards can either extend restrictions to co-conspirators or avoid alerting co-conspirators of the pending investigation by removing the lead suspect by means other than administrative leave, which may spark suspicion of an investigation. For example, the suspect could be sent away for a few days for training, removing the person from the workplace while not raising suspicions of those left behind who could cover their tracks.

Assemble the Investigation Team

Once efforts have been made to secure evidence and assets, the next step in the investigation is assembling the investigation team, a task generally performed by management. The use of external resources should be considered for high-profile fraud, with the benefits being access to specialized skills and the ability of external resources to stay removed from internal politics that could hamper either the investigation or the credibility of the outcome.

Fraud investigations that involve the CEO or the CFO would command the involvement of the board. Based on the experience of Vasant Ravel with infoGroup Inc., it is suggested that the board include outside resources as deemed necessary in the execution of its duties. In addition, the involvement of the CEO and CFO must be ruled out in forming the investigation team, to preserve the integrity of the investigation.

The exact composition of the investigation team varies based on an organization's size, structure, and resources. Typical team members on an investigation include the board and representatives from management, the investigations unit, and the internal audit, finance/accounting, legal, human resources, and investor relations departments. Who is involved and when they are involved is a matter to be determined by the board. A suggested division of responsibilities is outlined in Figure 10.1.

Regardless of the variations in team formation, legal counsel should be included in all fraud investigations. Legal counsel can ensure that work performed during the investigation is protected as confidential under the work-product rule. In addition, legal counsel can ensure that employee rights are respected with regards to investigation methods and during disciplinary measures that result from the investigation.

Respond to Findings

In response to the conclusions of a fraud investigation, consistency is critical. Significant damage to morale can be done when punishments differ for what appear to be equivalent infractions. Once an investigation has been concluded and a report issued, the organization must decide what it will do to punish perpetrators, recover losses, and reduce the likelihood of recurrence.

To set a strong moral tone in the organization, boards should consider a zero-tolerance policy in which all violations, regardless of dollar amount, are punished. Organizations that fail to punish smaller frauds tend to suffer from larger and larger frauds as the perceived opportunity to steal without punishment increases.

Boards also should look for ways to recover losses incurred by these violations. As for recovering resources, organizations may seek financial recovery through insurance or litigation. Insurers have a prescribed protocol for processing claims. Organizations also can pursue litigation, either as a criminal matter or through civil proceedings. Law enforcement may not take up cases of fraud for dollar amounts that fall below a predetermined limit. For example, many FBI units refer fraud cases below $1 million to local law enforcement.

Fraud-Risk Procedure	Board/Audit Committee	Internal Audit	Finance/Accounting	Management	Legal	Investigations Unit	Human Resources	Investor Relations
Receive Tips	SR	P						
Investigate Fraud Allegations		SR	S	S	SR	SR		
High-Profile Fraud Investigations	P	SR			P			
Law-Enforcement Liaison					SR	P		
Develop Fraud-Prevention Procedures		SR	SR	SR				
Consider Fraud Risk	SR	SR	SR	SR	SR	SR		
Investor/Public Relations			P					P
Risk Assessment	P	SR	SR	P				
Monitor Recoveries			P	S				
Test Controls		P						
Fraud Training		P					P	

P=Primary Responsibility; S=Secondary Responsibility; SR=Shared Responsibility

Figure 10.1   Fraud investigations: A suggested division of responsibilities.

There are merits to both criminal and civil prosecution. Civil proceedings offer organizations more control but lack the benefits of criminal investigations, which include improved investigative powers and use of government resources to investigate. Criminal investigations are not always best for organizations because they could render the suspect insolvent, making financial recovery for the organization impossible.

In reading the investigation report, joint efforts with the internal audit and finance/accounting departments should be undertaken to develop procedures that reduce the likelihood of repeat occurrences. If key mitigating controls are developed, the satisfactory performance of those controls should be tested and reported at the appropriate level of oversight, whether that be the head of internal audit, finance, or even the audit committee.

Conclude the Investigation

At the conclusion of every fraud investigation, documentation should be provided by the investigation team as to the resolution, which can include disciplinary action or referral to law enforcement. If the investigation is put on hold because of lack of evidence, a listing of desired documentation or some other trigger to reopen the investigation should be listed.

ACTION STEPS

▲ Ensure investigations at all levels demonstrate consistency, skepticism, authenticity, and credibility.

▲ Audit committees should get involved in the investigations that involve:

　◑ Financial reporting and disclosure obligations and accounting improprieties

　◑ Alleged diversions of company funds and/or inappropriate purchases by senior staff

　◑ Negligent contract administration

- ◑ Inadequate internal controls

- ◑ Suspicious market trading

- ◑ High dollar frauds

- ◑ Frauds involving senior management

▲ Provide input in the design of investigation protocols in the areas of receiving and evaluating complaints, preserving evidence for investigations involving senior staff, assembling the investigation team, and responding to findings.

The Need for CFO and CAE Succession Plans

Many organizations consider having a CEO succession plan an essential board function that serves to calm the markets by promising the continued sustainability of an organization's current economic performance. One need look no further than the public scrutiny the Apple board faced for a lack of a transparent CEO succession plan to replace the arguably irreplaceable Steve Jobs.

Despite the common well-accepted need for a CEO succession plan, the need for chief financial officer (CFO) and chief audit executive (CAE) succession plans is often overlooked. With the CFO serving as a popular choice to replace the CEO, a CEO succession plan may create a vacancy in the CFO role that must be addressed as part of a sound CEO succession plan. Even if an organization does not plan to use the CFO to replace the CEO, boards should have a CFO succession plan in place because CFO tenures have been steadily declining because of increased performances demand driven by increased regulatory pressure and persistent economic turmoil.

The Reason for Audit Committee Involvement in Succession Planning

The essential governance roles that the CFO and CAE serve in support of the audit committee mission suggest that the audit committee share a role alongside the CEO in selecting the CFO and CAE. The CFO, while serving as a major ally to the CEO, also provides the board an important counterpoint perspective to management directives by presenting multiple scenarios for any proposed plan. The CAE serves as a watchdog, ready to inform the board of significant deviations from agreed-upon controls and reporting practices.

While the input of the audit committee is more readily accepted by the CEO in the choice of replacing the CAE, the CEO may bristle at the involvement of the audit committee in the choice of CFO since the CEO may be used to making the choice independently of audit committee counsel. Many times the CEO brings along a CFO who shares a preexisting work relationship, increasing the fraud risks of collusion and override of management controls for which the audit committee must provide additional oversight.

To be mindful of CEO sentiments, the board may take a lesser role in the CFO hiring decisions, merely approving the hiring of the CFO based on the CEO's recommendations, while taking a primary role in CAE hiring decisions.

The Role of the CFO

The CFO is the top financial executive for an organization (smaller organizations, however, may give the title of controller or vice president of finance to the top financial executive). The CFO's duties are many and include serving as key adviser to the CEO, negotiating financing terms with banks, and representing the company to investors. Characteristics of organizations that benefit from the additional financial skills of a CFO include having revenues in excess of $5 million, more than 30 employees, the requirement for an external audit, and any imminent plans to go public.[11]

Reported tenures for CFOs are in the range of 4 to 12 years[12]; average director tenure comes in at just under 8 years.[13] Eighty-three percent of CFOs do not have a named successor, suggesting that most organizations have not planned for the exit of the person who holds that critical position. Nearly half of CFOs are promoted from within,[14] such as the controller, when vacancies occur.

The Role of the CAE

The CAE is the top internal auditor of an organization. Using the title of CAE rather than other titles such as lead auditor or internal audit manager speaks to the perceived importance of the role as bestowed by those in the organization charged with governance. The CAE serves as the key liaison to the board of directors and external auditors.

A rotational CAE model in which the top auditor position is selected from within the CFO department has become a popular trend, with big name organizations such as Coca-Cola, Home Depot, and General Electric subscribing to the rotational model. This model offers a fresh perspective to the audit functions of risk assessment and audit testing because career finance professionals bring with them an enhanced awareness of critical business operations than are available when the CAE comes from a strictly audit-based professional background. As an added bonus, internal audit recommendations may be more readily adopted because the message comes from a trusted colleague who was once a coworker in the finance department.

One shortcoming to the rotational CAE model is that the coveted independence of the internal audit function may be compromised because of the preexisting connections when the CAE comes from the CFO department. While this risk is inherent to the rotational CAE model, audit committee members can adapt their skepticism to adjust to any perceived conflicts.[15]

Irrespective of the source of the CAE, care must be taken to maintain the quality that comes with experience by promoting stability within the internal audit function, with a target minimum tenure for CAEs of no less than five years recommended.

ACTION STEPS

⋏ Develop a succession plan for the CFO and CAE roles.

⋏ Be sensitive to CEO direction in the choice of CFO, with the board seeking influence over the choice of CFO rather than exerting veto power.

▲ Take an active role in selecting the CAE. Consider the rotational model for the CAE role.

▲ Be vigilant about the increased fraud risk for collusion and management override of controls for C-suite choices who share a preexisting relationship with the CEO.

Conclusion

Perhaps no single business topic is more hotly debated than governance. Clearly there are different perspectives, cultures, and operating environments. No one set of principles is necessarily the best fit for all organizations. That said, simplicity in definitions and goals should be the objective rather than complex legalistic policies and procedures. Toward this end, here is a summary of our top action items and supporting considerations.

Forty Key Action Items

Nominate Independent Directors

1. Directors must keep the shareholders' interests at the forefront: Audit committee members must represent shareholders' interests rather than the CEO's interest. This is a necessity, since a key duty of the audit committee is to independently monitor the executive team, especially regarding financial reporting. Indeed, the board of directors and its committees are legally and ethically required to protect the people who own the company, or in the case of nonprofits, funding sources and the nonprofit objectives. However, this

core purpose should not preclude directors and board committees from also providing management with knowledgeable advice and connections.

2. Recruit audit committee members who are not afraid to voice dissent: Since the audit committee culture should be injected with heavy doses of constructive skepticism, it is critical to nominate directors to the audit committee who will be vocal in dealing with controversy and difficult matters.

3. Seek diversity on the board and its committees: This means recruiting directors from different industries, professional competencies, age groups, and genders. Such diversity also appeals with key stakeholders.

4. Strive for a well-crafted definition of independence: Independence is largely the willingness to challenge the CEO without biases in the service of the shareholders' best interest.

Establish a Culture of Action

5. Be deliberate in defining an organizational culture through training and education: While tactical nominations serve as the core of any audit committee culture, training and education on fiduciary duties is a must.

6. Strive for a culture that is informed, active, and maintains an open but challenging relationship with the CEO and external auditor: Board and audit committee cultures can take on many different styles, but the ideal culture must be based on action and constructive skepticism.

7. Avoid a board and audit committee culture dominated by the CEO: This is in essence a conflict of interest since a primary purpose of the board and audit committee is to provide oversight over this individual.

8. Treat no subject as off-limits: There should be no sacred cows that are considered untouchable at audit committee meetings.

Evaluate the Audit Committee

9. Insist on an audit committee evaluation at least once every two years: A well-crafted and well-executed evaluation pays high dividends in helping steer the audit committee to success.

10. Focus on substance rather than strictly form: Too often, companies evaluate legal compliance through their audit committee evaluation rather than the essence of what really counts, such as culture, activities regarding management oversight, and risk awareness. While compliance with regulatory rules and regulations as well as with the audit committee charter are important, they should not be the sole focus for audit committee evaluations.

11. Be brutally honest: Remember that it is not just the structure but rather the people who count the most with regard to evaluating board committees. This makes it very challenging to candidly evaluate an audit committee's performance since friendships and other biases frequently enter the picture.

12. Consider outside legal counsel or consultants to lead the evaluation: This usually leads to a much stronger evaluation process with greater independence.

Direct the External Audit

13. It all begins with education: Every audit committee member should be well versed on the external audit process. This includes understanding the role, standards, and tendencies of external auditors. The audit committee must be astute as to what the external auditor can and cannot do for the organization.

14. Understand and practice a risk-based approach in fulfilling duties: Taking such an approach simply means assigning resources to where the greatest risks reside to reduce control deficiencies identified in the risk-assessment process. External audit standards are grounded in this philosophy.

15. Avoid overreliance on the external audit to detect errors and irregularities: While the auditor considers ICFR risks, understand that

it is the board, audit committee, and management who are primarily responsible for considering and acting upon financial statement risks since they own the controls. A mistake many organizations make is overrelying on the external audit.

16. Don't settle for anything short of the unvarnished truth: Demand and deliver candid communications from and to your external auditors. Remind them that they work for the audit committee and not management.

Scrutinize the Financial Statements

17. Focus on the common types of financial and disclosure misstatements: These include overstated revenues, understated expenses, inflated assets, and misleading disclosures in the footnotes and in management discussion and analysis (as required for public companies). In its investigations, the SEC has cited these areas the most for corrective actions.

18. Understand materiality: According to SEC Staff Accounting Bulletin No. 99, "The omission or misstatement of an item in a financial report is material if, in the light of surrounding circumstances, the magnitude of the item is such that it is probable that the judgment of a reasonable person relying upon the report would have been changed or influenced by the inclusion or correction of the item."[1] One should consider quantitative and qualitative aspects when determining materiality.

19. Consider management integrity: Evaluate the likelihood of misleading financial statements based on the integrity of managers, including their willingness to make significant adjustments or adverse disclosures.

20. Raise your professional skepticism level consistent with pressures that exist for management to issue misleading financial statements or disclosures: Audit committee members can gain a pulse of these pressures by keeping tabs on industry fraud, the organization's incentive program, and the degree of opportunities and rationalizations that may exist.

Leverage Internal Audit and Outside Resources

21. Position internal audit resources as key advisers: Internal audit resources offer valuable insights and can provide assurance resources to help the board and audit committee fulfill their duties.

22. Demand independence: Insist upon, and evaluate, the independence and objectivity of the internal audit function. This helps ensure the comfort level of audit committee members' reliance on internal audit findings. Objectivity relates to factors that might influence an individual, such as the chief audit executive, to not report inaccurate or incomplete information, thus not allowing the board members to reach an appropriate conclusion. If the internal audit function is under management's marching orders, independence and objectivity are likely impaired.

23. Take control over the allocation of internal audit resources: Provide sufficient resources to the internal audit function to ensure that it can move beyond a compliance-centric focus and address operational, financial, and strategic initiatives.

24. Utilize surprise audits: Ideally, the auditee should not be aware of the internal audit approach, testing thresholds, and precise sample of items to be tested until they are ready to be pulled for testing. Audit procedures and timing should also be changed from time to time. The audit committee should ensure that the CAE proposes and implements an audit program that meets the spirit of surprise audits.

Satisfy Regulators and Other Stakeholders

25. Be familiar with shareholders, communities, employees, customers, suppliers, creditors, and regulators: Not knowing them can be a ticking time bomb to the business in the event key stakeholder objectives are not addressed.

26. Initiate more communication between directors, shareholders, and other stakeholders: Directors must listen both inside and outside the boardroom. This is particularly important with creditors, employees, and customers.

27. Identify and understand applicable key regulations: All organizations are subject to some degree of regulation. Utilize a risk-based approach in understanding those that can potentially be the most harmful because of noncompliance. Remember that ignorance of rules and regulations is not a sound alibi.

28. Be vigilant in ensuring that the record-retention policy of the organization is comprehensive and current: Destroying records before required due dates jeopardizes a company's defense in fighting off adverse litigation. Likewise, retaining business records beyond legal time frames subjects the company to having discoverable documents that otherwise would not exist.

Address Risk Proactively

29. Avoid losing a trusted reputation, which is a great risk: It takes decades to build a solid reputation, yet it can be lost with a single corporate lapse.

30. Avoid a check-box mentality in addressing risk: Checklists can be used as a starting point, but organizations should go further to customize the evaluation tool to best fit their needs. Audit committee risk efforts should be grounded in the applicable regulatory environment, company strategy, and executive performance.

31. Consider information flows and decision-making processes in the risk assessment: Be careful of management providing mounds of irrelevant data to camouflage unpleasant realities.

32. Keep the topic of risk on every audit committee agenda: In addition to ICFR risks, keep operational and compliance risks alive by discussing them at audit committee meetings. Also discuss these risks with the external and internal auditors to gain their perspectives.

Spearhead Fraud-Deterrence Initiatives

33. Ensure that an effective whistle-blower hotline is in place: This has proven to be a very cost-effective tool in preventing and

detecting fraud. In addition to inviting employees to use it, open it up to customers, vendors, and other stakeholders.

34. Challenge management to segregate duties: As a general rule, the initiating, authorizing, receiving/custody, recording, and reconciling of transactions and balances should be segregated. While this can be a challenge for smaller organizations, strive for creative solutions to maximize segregation of duties.

35. Actively review financial results, including ratio analytics, and challenge management explanations of unexpected results: This is a powerful way to detect fraud. It also alerts management that someone is watching. The perception of detection is a very powerful element in a control environment.

36. Leverage continuous monitoring through technology: Software programs are becoming more powerful and less costly, so they can be highly effective in preventing and detecting fraud. Task your internal audit function to work with the IT function and independent advisers to realize a reasonable degree of automated controls within the ICFR.

Expect the Unexpected

37. Be proactive in setting up a crisis-management team before it is needed: Ideally this entails a written plan with definitive steps and identified resources defined.

38. Define potential scenarios and resources for conducting investigations: Don't wait until an investigation is needed, but rather have a course of action mapped out for a variety of plausible possibilities. The audit committee should be initiating internal investigations in many cases.

39. Institute succession planning: The audit committee should plan for the expected and emergency successions of the CFO and the CAE. Likewise, the potential for a rapid change in external audit firms should be considered.

40. Always be on the lookout for collusion and executive management override of controls: Never let your guard down on this front; many frauds could have been prevented and detected through more vigilance.

Notes

Introduction

1. U.S. Securities and Exchange Commission, *2011 Performance and Accountability Report*, 13, http://www.sec.gov/about/secpar2011.shtml, accessed January 9, 2013.

2. Sonora Resources Corp., *Form 10-K* as filed to the SEC on January 27, 2012, annual report with a comprehensive overview of the company, 28.

3. Buka Ventures Inc., *Form 10-K* as filed to the SEC on January 27, 2012, annual report with a comprehensive overview of the company, 25.

Chapter 1: Nominate Independent Directors

1. Financial Accounting Standards Board (FASB) U.S. GAAP, Codification of Accounting Standards, *Topic 850: Related Party Disclosures,* AU334.02, Source SAS No. 45.

2. New York Stock Exchange, *Listed Company Manual*, Sec. 303A.02, "Independence Tests," www.nysemanual.nyse.com, accessed January 9, 2013.

3. New York Stock Exchange, *Listed Company Manual*, Commentary to Sec. 303A.02(a), "Independence Tests," www.nysemanual.nyse.com, accessed January 9, 2013.

4. Sarbanes-Oxley Act of 2002, Sec. 407, "Disclosure of Audit Committee Financial Expert," [15USC7265].

5. Ibid.

6. New York Stock Exchange, *Listed Company Manual*, Sec. 303A.07 (a), "Audit Committee Additional Requirements," available at www.nysemanual.nyse.com, accessed January 9, 2013.

7. Renee Adams and Daniel Ferreira, "Women in the Boardroom and Their Impact on Governance and Performance," *Journal of Financial Economics* 94(2) (2009), 291-309.

8. *2011 Spencer Stuart Board Index*, Spencer Stuart, 6.

9. Ibid.

10. Ibid., 38.

11. Ibid., 14.

Chapter 2: Establish a Culture of Action

1. *Pereira v. Cogan*, 294 BR 449—Dist. Court, SD New York 2003, http://scholar.google.com/scholar_case?case=6053684912927476907&hl=en&as_sdt=2&as_vis=1&oi=scholarr, accessed January 9, 2013.

2. Dorsey & Whitney LLP, Minneapolis Office, "Fiduciary Duties and the Zone of Insolvency—Pereira v. Cogan Reminds Directors of Private Corporations of Their Duties to Shareholders and Creditors," September 29, 2003, http://www.martindale.com/professional-liability-law/article_Dorsey-Whitney-LLP_33474.htm, accessed January 9, 2013.

3. U.S. District Court, Northern District of Illinois, Eastern Division, Case: 1:09-cv-01538 Document #: 149 Filed: 05/17/11.

Chapter 3: Evaluate the Audit Committee

1. *Spencer Stuart*, 33.

2. Ibid., 31.

3. New York Stock Exchange, *Listed Company Manual*, Sec. 303A.07 (b)(ii), "Audit Committee Additional Requirements," available at www.nysemanual.nyse.com, accessed January 9, 2013.

4. *Spencer Stuart*, 32.

5. From Georgia Nelson, Center for Executive Women, Northwestern University, in phone conversation with the authors, February 16, 2012.

6. *Spencer Stuart*, 33.

Chapter 4: Direct the External Audit

1. U.S. District Court, Central District of California, *In Re New Century*, Case No. 2:07-cv-00931-DDP, August 17, 2010.

2. Public Company Accounting Oversight Board, Auditing Standard No. 5, para. 79; and American Institute of Certified Public Accountants, Auditing Standards Board, AU Sec. 325, para. No. 5.

3. Auditing Standards Board, Statement on Auditing Standards No. 114, "The Auditor's Communication with Those Charged with Governance," AU 380.03.

4. Ibid., AU 380.23.

5. Public Company Accounting Oversight Board, Auditing Standard No. 12, "Identifying and Assessing Risks of Material Misstatement," para. 56(b), effec-

tive pursuant to SEC Release No. 34-63606, File No. PCAOB-2010-01 (December 23, 2010).

6. Sarbanes-Oxley Act of 2002, Sec. 201(a), "Services Outside the Scope of Practices for Auditors," [116 STAT.115-116].

7. SEC, final rule on "Strengthening the Commission's Requirements Regarding Auditor Independence," per Release #33-8183, January 23, 2003.

Chapter 5: Scrutinize the Financial Statements

1. H. Schilit and J. Perler, *Financial Shenanigans* (New York City: McGraw Hill, 2010), 6.

2. Alex Berenson, "Computer Associates Restates Timing of $2.2 Billion in Sales," *New York Times*, April 27, 2004, http://www.nytimes.com/2004/04/27/business/computer-associates-restates-timing-of-2.2-billion-in-sales.html, accessed January 9, 2013.

3. "Florafax International Reports Record Revenues for Second Quarter; Fiscal Year-End and First Quarter Results Restated," *Business Wire*, April 15, 1999, http://www.thefreelibrary.com/Florafax+International+Reports+Record+Revenues+for+Second+Quarter%3B...-a054387265, accessed January 9, 2013.

4. Patricia M. Dechow, Weili Ge, Chad R. Larson, and Richard G. Sloan, "Predicting Material Accounting Manipulations," *Contemporary Accounting Research, Forthcoming AAA 2008 Financial Accounting and Reporting Section (FARS) Paper*, May 29, 2008, 17.

5. "How to Hide $3.8 Billion in Expenses," *Bloomberg Businessweek*, July 8, 2002, http://www.businessweek.com/stories/2002-07-07/how-to-hide-3-dot-8-billion-in-expenses, accessed January 9, 2013.

6. Dechow, et al., "Predicting Material Accounting Manipulations," Table 1 Panel F: Type of msistatements identified by the SEC in the AAER, 57.

7. Hollis Skaife and Daniel Wangerin, "Target Financial Reporting Quality and M&A Deals That Go Bust," March 16, 2012, http://ssrn.com/abstract= 1823727, accessed January 9, 2013.

8. SEC, "SEC Sues Former CEO and CFO of Gemstar-TV Guide for Financial Fraud Scheme," 2003-75, June 19, 2003, http://www.sec.gov/news/press/2003-75.htm, accessed January 25, 2013.

9. Sunita Goel, Jagdish Gongolly, Sue R. Faerman, and Ozlem Uzuner, "Can Linguistic Predictors Detect Fraudulent Financial Filings?" American Accounting Association, *Journal of Emerging Technologies in Accounting* 7 (2010), 39, Table 6: Simple Surface Features for a Sample Fraudulent and Nonfraudulent Annual Report.

10. Ibid., 33, Table 3: List of Discriminating Words Panel B: Ranking of the Top 25 Discriminating Words by Information Gain for the Predicting Levels of Fraud.

11. Natasha Burns and Simia Kedia, "Executive Option Exercises and Financial Misreporting," July 2006, http://www.kedia.rutgers.edu/wp/exerpaper _july06.pdf, accessed March 4, 2013.

12. Daniel Bergstresser and Thomas Philippon, "CEO Incentives and Earnings Management," *Journal of Financial Economics* 80 (2006), http://www.kedia .rutgers.edu/wp/exerpaper_july06.pdf, accessed March 4, 2013.

13. Merle Erickson, Michelle Hanlon, and Edward Maydew, "Is There a Link Between Executive Compensation and Accounting Fraud?" February 2004.

14. Bill Saporito, "How Fastow Helped Enron Fall," Time.com, February 20, 2002, http://www.time.com/time/business/article/0,8599,201871,00.html, accessed January 29, 2013.

15. SEC Staff Accounting Bulletin: *No. 101—Revenue Recognition in Financial Statements*, 17 CFR Part 211.

16. Microsoft 2011 *Form 10-K* filing.

Chapter 6: Leverage Internal Audit and Outside Resources

1. Christine Petrovits, Catherine Shakespeare, and Aimee Shih, "The Causes and Consequences of Internal Control Problems in Nonprofits," April 2009, http://pbfea2005.rutgers.edu/20thFEA/AccountingPapers/Session4/ Petrovits,%20Shakespeare,%20and%20Shih.pdf, accessed February 16, 2013.

2. New York Stock Exchange, *Listed Company Manual*, Sec. 303A.07(iii)(E), "Audit Committee Additional Requirements," http://nysemanual.nyse.com/ LCMTools/PlatformViewer.asp?searched=1&selectednode=chp%5F1%5F4% 5F3%5F8&CiRestriction=internal+AND+audit+AND+function&manual= %2Flcm%2Fsections%2Flcm%2Dsections%2F, accessed January 29, 2013.

3. Ibid.

4. Institute of Internal Auditors, Standards & Guidance—International Professional Practices Framework, Glossary, https://na.theiia.org/standards-guidance/ mandatory-guidance/Pages/Standards-Glossary.aspx, accessed January 13, 2013.

5. Ibid.

6. Institute of Internal Auditors, *International Standards for the Professional Practice of Internal Auditing,* https://na.theiia.org/standards-guidance/mandatory-guidance/ Pages/Standards.aspx, accessed January 13, 2013.

7. American Strategic Minerals Corp—VNTSD, *Form 10-K* as filed to the SEC on December 14, 2011, 13.

8. Hollis Ashbaugh Skaife, Daniel W. Collins, William R. Kinney Jr., and Ryan LaFond, "The Effect of SOX Internal Control Deficiencies on Firm Risk and Cost of Equity," *Journal of Accounting Research,* vol. 47:1 (March 2009), 35.

9. Public Company Accounting Oversight Board, *2010 Inspection of Deloitte & Touche LLP*, December 7, 2011, 18, http://pcaobus.org/Inspections/Reports/ Documents/2011_Deloitte.pdf, accessed January 13, 2013.

Chapter 7: Satisfy Regulators and Other Stakeholders

1. "Apple Criticized for China Supply Chain Pollution," Reuters, August 31, 2011, http://www.reuters.com/article/2011/08/31/us-apple-china-idUSTRE 77U4M620110831, accessed February 16, 2013; and "Wal-Mart's Pork Scandal Highlights Struggles in China," Reuters, October 14, 2011, http://www.reuters.com/article/2011/10/14/walmart-china-idUSL3E7LD1P 220111014, accessed February 16, 2013.

2. National Bureau of Economic Research, http://www.nber.org/digest/apr07/w12354.html, accessed January 13, 2013. There are just under 5,200 companies listed between the NASDAQ and NYSE (www.topforeignstocks.com).

3. Jonathan Spicer and Rachelle Younglai, "Single Trade Helped Spark May's Flash Crash," Reuters, Oct 1, 2010, http://www.reuters.com/article/2010/10/02/us-flash-idUSTRE69040W20101002, accessed January 14, 2013.

4. Mary Shapiro, speech titled "Looking Ahead and Moving Forward," February 5, 2010, http://www.sec.gov/news/speech/2010/spch020510mls.htm, accessed January 13, 2013.

5. Committee of Sponsoring Organizations, *Internal Control-Integrated Framework*, http://www.coso.org/documents/coso_framework_body_v6.pdf, accessed January 13, 2013.

6. COSO, *Internal Control–Integrated Framework*, 2-3, http://www.coso.org/documents/Internal%20Control-Integrated%20Framework.pdf, accessed January 14, 2013.

7. Transparency International, *Global Corruption Report 2009*, executive overview, 2.

8. "Five Travel Expenses Related FCPA Violations," http://www.secwhistle blowerprogram.org/SEC-Whistleblower-Blog/bid/52066/Five-travel -expense-related-FCPA-violations, accessed January 14, 2013.

9. Dionne Searcey, "Former Enforcer Sees Looming Fight," *Wall Street Journal,* March 17, 2011, http://online.wsj.com/article/SB100014240527487043965045762049441736 67866.html, accessed January 13, 2013.

10. Law 360, "The Pitfalls of Shifting DOJ Policies" July 21, 2011, http://www .snrdenton.com/pdf/Law360%20The%20Pitfalls%20Of%20Shifting%20DOJ% 20Policies.pdf, accessed January 14, 2013.

Chapter 8: Address Risk Proactively

1. New York Stock Exchange, Final NYSE Corporate Governance Rules, 2004, 12, http://www.nyse.com/pdfs/finalcorpgovrules.pdf, accessed January 13, 2013.

2. Standard & Poor's, *Progress Report: Integrating Enterprise Risk-Management Analysis into Corporate Credit Ratings*, July 22, 2009, 3, http://internalaudits.duke.edu/documents/articles_archive/Progress_Report7 _22_09.pdf, accessed January 13, 2013.

3. Public Company Accounting Oversight Board, Release No. 2007-005A, Auditing Standard No. 5: "An Audit of Internal Control Over Financial Reporting That Is Integrated with an Audit of Financial Statements," June 12, 2007, A1-8-Standard.

4. Association of Certified Fraud Examiners, 2012 *Report to the Nations on Occupational Fraud and Abuse*, 12.

5. Ibid., 52.

6. Ibid., 11.

7. Mark S. Beasley, Joseph V. Carcello, Dana R. Hermanson, and Terry L. Neal, *Fraudulent Financial Reporting: 1998–2007—An Analysis of U.S. Public Companies*, Committee of Sponsoring Organizations, 2010, III, Executive Summary.

8. Committee of Sponsoring Organizations, *Strengthening Enterprise Risk-Management for Strategic Advantage*, 2009, 7.

9. Alix Stuart, "The True Cost of Going Public," *CFO Magazine*, December 1, 2011, http://www.cfo.com/article.cfm/14609551, accessed January 13, 2013.

10. Jim Collins, *Good to Great* (New York City: Harper Business, 2001), 10.

11. Peter Drucker, *The Daily Drucker* (New York City: Harper Collins, 2004), 7.

12. Donald Trump, *Never Give Up* (Hoboken, NJ: Wiley, 2008), 166.

Chapter 9: Spearhead Fraud-Deterrence Initiatives

1. Association of Certified Fraud Examiners, 2012 *Report to the Nations*, 4.

2. *Fraudulent Financial Reporting*, III, Executive Summary, http://www.coso.org/documents/COSOFRAUDSTUDY2010_001.pdf, accessed January 13, 2013.

3. *Report to the Nations*, 2010, 4.

4. "Great Numbers, Weak Governance: Is AIG a Special Case?" *Bloomberg Businessweek*, October 7, 2002, http://www.businessweek.com/magazine/content/02_40/b3802009.htm.

5. Elaine Henry, Elizabeth A. Gordon, Brad Reed, and Timothy Louwers, "The Role of Related Party Transactions in Fraudulent Financial Reporting," 3, Table 8, 38, June 2007, http://ssrn.com/abstract=993532, accessed January 13, 2013.

6. U.S. Attorney's Office, "Managing Director of Bank's Investment Company Convicted of Embezzling over $571,000," news release, March 22, 2011.

7. Securities and Exchange Commission, "SEC Charges Adelphia and Rigas Family with Massive Financial Fraud," available at www.sec.gov, 2002-110, accessed January 13, 2013.

8. "10 Worst Corporate Boards of the Decade," *The Daily Beast*, caption for Adelphia, http://www.thedailybeast.com/galleries/2011/09/23/10-worst-corporate-boards-photos.html, accessed January 13, 2013.

9. "AMR CEO Arpey Received $5.2 Million in 2010, Despite Carrier's Losses," http://blogs.star-telegram.com/sky_talk/2011/04/amr-ceo-arpey-received

-52-million-in-2010-despite-carriers-losses.html, accessed January 13, 2013; "Despite Losses, American Airlines CEO's Compensation Climbs," *Star-Telegram*, April 21, 2011, http://blogs.star-telegram.com/sky_talk/2011/04/amr-ceo-arpey-received-52-million-in-2010-despite-carriers-losses.html, accessed February 16, 2013.

10. "Manulife CEO Paid C$9.3 Mln Despite 2010 Net Loss," Reuters, March 25, 2011, http://www.reuters.com/article/2011/03/25/manulife-ceo-salary-idUSN2527802520110325, accessed January 13, 2013.

11. "Top Warner Execs 2010 Pay Increased Despite Revenue Losses," Billboard.biz, January 20, 2011, http://www.billboard.biz/bbbiz/industry/record-labels/top-warner-execs-2010-pay-increased-despite-1004139709.story, accessed January 13, 2013.

12. United for a Fair Economy and Institute for Policy Studies, "The Ratio of Average CEO and Worker Pay in the US," 1, http://www.faireconomy.org/files/ExecutiveExcess2006.pdf, accessed January 13, 2013.

13. Mercer Survey of 350 large industrial and service firms conducted for the *Wall Street Journal*, "The Ratio of Average CEO Compensation and Minimum Wage Worker in the US, 1965–2005," http://www.heritageinstitute.com/governance/compensation.htm#The_Ratio_of_Average_CEO_and_Worker, accessed January 13, 2013.

14. Reports vary, with the multiplier ranging from 5 to 1 to 9 to 1.

15. Institute for Fraud Prevention, Chad Albrecht, Mary-Jo Kranacher, and Steve Albrecht, "Asset Misappropriation Research White Paper for the Institute for Fraud Prevention," 14, http://www.theifp.org/research-grants/IFP-Whitepaper-5.pdf, accessed January 13, 2013.

16. ACFE, 2012 *Report to the Nations*, 12, http://www.acfe.com/uploadedFiles/ACFE_Website/Content/rttn/2012-report-to-nations.pdf, accessed January 14, 2013.

17. *2010 U.S. Intellectual Property Enforcement Coordinator Annual Report on Intellectual Property Enforcement*, 32, http://www.whitehouse.gov/sites/default/files/omb/IPEC/ipec_annual_report_feb2011.pdf, accessed January 13, 2013.

18. Ibid., 9-60.

19. Mark S. Beasley, Joseph V. Carcello, Dana R. Hermanson, and Terry L. Neal, *Fraudulent Financial Reporting: 1998–2007—An Analysis of U.S. Public Companies,* Committee of Sponsoring Organizations, 2010, III, Executive Summary.

20. Ibid., 4.

21. SEC, "Waste Management Founder, Five Other Former Top Officers Sued for Massive Fraud," http://www.sec.gov/news/headlines/wastemgmt6.htm, accessed January 13, 2013.

22. *Most Improved Boards, Bloomberg Business*, October 7, 2002, http://www.businessweek.com/magazine/content/02_40/b3802006.htm.

23. *Fraudulent Financial Reporting*, Executive Summary III.

24. *Report to the Nations*, 17.

25. *Tides v. Boeing*, U.S.. Court of Appeals for the Ninth Circuit, May 3, 2011, No. 10-35238, http://www.ca9.uscourts.gov/datastore/opinions/2011/05/03/10-35238.pdf.

26. After several hearings, the Merit Systems Protection Board in 2011 ruled that McLean was not retaliated against.

27. Ethics Resource Center, 2009 National Business Ethics Survey, *Retaliation: The Cost to Your Company and Its Employees*, 10, http://ethics.org/files/u5/Retaliation.pdf, accessed January 13, 2013.

28. Ernst & Young, Vincent Walden, and Michael Sherrod, "Viewpoint—Breaking the Status Quo: Moving Beyond Traditional E-Mail Review," *Fraud Watch*, January 2011, http://www.ey.com/IN/en/Services/Assurance/Fraud-Investigation-Dispute-Services/Fraud-Watch-Viewpoint, accessed January 13, 2013.

29. Ibid.

30. Ethisphere.Com, *World's Most Ethical Companies*, http://ethisphere.com/2011-worlds-most-ethical-companies/, January 13, 2013.

31. Ethics Resource Center, 2005 National Business Ethics Survey, presentation, dated 11/15/2005, slide 4 http://www.dau.mil/conferences/presentations/2005_PEO_SYSCOM/PEO%20Tuesday-Web/Ethics%20Panel%20-%20Epstein.pdf, accessed January 13, 2013.

32. University of California Office of the President, *Understanding Internal Controls*, https://financial.ucsc.edu/pages/management_separationofduties.aspx, accessed January 13, 2013.

33. Vermont State Auditor, *Segregation of Duties*, http://auditor.vermont.gov/sites/auditor/files/Segregation_of_Duties.pdf.

34. SEC, "SEC Charges Officer and Employee of Milwaukee Corporation in $30 Million Embezzlement, SEC versus Sujata Sachdeva and Julie Mulvaney," Civil Case No. 10-CV-0747, USDC, E.D., Wisc., Accounting and Auditing Enforcement Release No. 3180/September 1, 2010, http://www.sec.gov/litigation/litreleases/2010/lr21640.htm.

35. 10-K filing, Koss Corp, June 30, 2010, http://www.sec.gov/Archives/edgar/data/56701/000110465910049173/a10-17957_110k.htm, Name and Title section, accessed February 16, 2013.

Chapter 10: Expect the Unexpected

1. Ben Protess and Andrew Ross Sorkin, "Sokol, Buffett and the Lubrizol Trades," Dealb%k, http://dealbook.nytimes.com/2011/03/31/sokol-and-the-lubrizol-trades/, accessed January 13, 2013.

2. Andrew Ross Sorkin, "Buffett Lets the Facts Bury Sokol," May 2, 2011, Dealb%l, http://dealbook.nytimes.com/2011/05/02/warren-buffett-lets-the-facts-bury-sokol/, accessed January 13, 2013.

3. Paul Sonne, Jeanne Whalen, and Bruce Orwall, "New Issues Emerge for News Corp. in Britain," *Wall Street Journal*, August 17, 2011, http://online.wsj.com/article/SB10001424053111903480904576511963847040354.html, accessed January 13, 2013.

4. Christine Schwen, "Murdoch Shutting Down News of the World; But That Won't Solve His Problems," NewsCorpWatch, July 7, 2011, http://newscorpwatch.org/blog/201107070024, accessed January 13, 2013.

5. Keith F. Higgins, "A Cautionary Tale for Audit Committee Chairs?" Harvard Law School Forum on Corporate Governance and Financial Regulation, April 8, 2010, http://blogs.law.harvard.edu/corpgov/2010/04/08/a-cautionary-tale-for-audit-committee-chairs/, accessed January 13, 2013.

6. SEC, "SEC Charges Military Body Armor Supplier and Former Outside Directors with Accounting Fraud," 2011-52, http://www.sec.gov/news/press/2011/2011-52.htm, accessed January 13, 2013.

7. Michael Cohn, "Body Armor Execs Settle Accounting Fraud Charges," *Accounting Today*, November 10, 2011, http://www.accountingtoday.com/news/Body-Armor-Execs-DHB-Point-Blank-Settle-Accounting-Fraud-Charges-60767-1.html, accessed January 13, 2013.

8. "SEC Charges Military Body Armor Supplier and Former Outside Directors with Accounting Fraud."

9. SEC, "SEC Enforcement Division Produces Record Results in Safeguarding Investors and Markets," 2011-234, http://www.sec.gov/news/press/2011/2011-234.htm, accessed January 13, 2013.

10. SEC, "Fighting Financial Fraud," http://www.sec.gov/news/press/2009/2009-249-fact-sheet.htm, accessed January 13, 2013.

11. "How to Hire a Chief Financial Officer," *Inc.*, February 16, 2010, http://www.inc.com/guides/hiring-a-chief-financial-officer-cfo.html, accessed January 13, 2013.

12. Jerry Bostelman, Financial Executive International, "Market-Proofing Your Career," May 21, 2012, http://www.financialexecutives.org/KenticoCMS/getattachment/Events/materials/Summit12/Presentation-Library/Brkfst3_Market-Proofing-Your-Career.pdf.aspx, accessed January 13, 2013; WebCPA, "CFO tenure appears to be lengthening," February 10, 2010, http://www.accountingtoday.com/news/CFO-Tenure-Lengthening-53255-1.html, accessed January 13, 2013.

13. *2011 Spencer Stuart Board Index*, 18, http://www.corpgov.deloitte.com/binary/com.epicentric.contentmanagement.servlet.ContentDeliveryServlet/FinFin/Documents/Home/2011%20US%20Spencer%20Stuart%20Board%20Index_Spencer%20Stuart_110711.pdf, accessed January 3, 2013.

14. Julia Homer, "Good Grooming: Why So Few CFOs Have Picked a Successor," *CFO Magazine*, November 1, 2007, http://www.cfo.com/article.cfm/ 10046497/c_10051145, accessed January 13, 2013.

15. Richard Chambers, "The Rotational CAE Model: Is It Good for Internal Auditing?" Chambers on the Profession, Internal Auditor, February 19, 2009, http://www.theiia.org/blogs/chambers/index.cfm/post/The%20Rotational% 20CAE%20Model:%20Is%20it%20Good%20for%20Internal%20Auditing, accessed February 16, 2013.

Conclusion

1. SEC Staff Accounting Bulletin: *No. 99—Materiality*, http://www.sec.gov/ interps/account/sab99.htm, accessed January 13, 2013.

INDEX